# WAR
## ON
# AMERICA
## SEEN FROM THE
## INDIAN OCEAN

by
James R. Mancham

D1446817

PARAGON HOUSE
St. Paul, Minnesota

First Edition, 2001

Published in the United States by
Paragon House
2700 University Avenue West
St. Paul, MN 55114

Copyright © 2002 by James R. Mancham

All rights reserved. No part of this book may be reproduced, in any form, without written permission from the publishers, unless by a reviewer who wishes to quote brief passages.

Cover image: Demonstrators burning the American flag and an effigy of U.S. President Bush in front of the U.S. Embassy compound in Kabul, Afghanistan. Courtesy of AP/Wide World Photos.

Manufactured in the United States of America.

Library of Congress Cataloging-in-Publishing data

Mancham, James R., 1939–
    War on America: seen from the Indian Ocean / by James R. Mancham.—1st ed.
        p. cm.
    ISBN 1-55778-815-4
        1. United States—Foreign public opinion. 2. United States—Foreign relations—Public opinion. 3. September 11 Terrorist Attacks, 2001—Public opinion. 4. Public opinion—Indian Ocean Region. 5. Public opinion—Seychelles. 6. Mancham, James R., 1939– 7. Presidents—Seychelles—Biography. I. Title.

E169.12.M23 2002
327.73—dc21

                                                            2001058826


10 9 8 7 6 5 4 3 2 1

For current information about all releases from Paragon House,
visit the web site at http://www.paragonhouse.com

# CONTENTS

# CHAPTER ONE

# WAR ON AMERICA
# CHALLENGES U.S. FOREIGN POLICY

GLACIS-SUR-MER, MAHÉ, SEYCHELLES—TUESDAY, SEPTEMBER 11, 2001. It was about 5:00 P.M.—Time to close the office and let the staff go. I was going through some pieces of poetry I had written years ago. One particularly struck me. "This green world—this clean world is a mighty good my friend. And if we only look for it, this world is full of fun. Smiles there are for every tear—so why should we be vexed? But let us build up happiness—to treasure in the next."

Suddenly my direct telephone rang—I picked it up. It was my daughter, Caroline Cooper, in Orlando, Florida on the line. "Daddy please switch on CNN—some terrible things have happened to the World Trade Center in New York City. I just can't believe it."

She was in a terrible state of shock.

I have a TV set in the room next to my office. In today's global village right here in the middle of the Indian Ocean, we are able to access CNN on a twenty-four-hour basis. In no time I was watching CNN Breaking News—an airplane had "crashed" into the first tower of the World Trade Center. Was it an accident? Was it foul play? I remained glued to the TV screen, and suddenly I saw the second plane crashing itself into the other tower as the former burnt into red, raw flames. Was I dreaming or was it real? I could not believe what I was seeing. I stayed glued to the screen and observed the development of the most horrendous and impactful drama I could have ever imagined.

Millions all over the United States and hundreds of millions all over the world were, like me, able to witness the attacks on WTC in New York City and the Pentagon in Washington, D.C., thanks to modern technology that is mostly in the control and ownership of corporations in one city of the United States of America or another.

Caroline telephoned another time. This time she was in tears—and her voice betrayed a state of fear.

"Daddy, Daddy what is becoming to our beautiful America? Who are those people who hate us so much as to wish so much destruction on us at the expense of their own lives? Daddy, Daddy I cannot really understand it."

I comforted her as much as I could.

Caroline was born in the Seychelles but became a U.S. Citizen after moving to Florida with her mother in the seventies when her mother and I were divorced. She has a beautiful five-year-old daughter, Lauren Cooper, who came on the line during the second call.

"Grandpa, Mama is crying because New York is on fire. When are you coming to see us? We love you Grandpa."

I became tearful myself as I put the telephone down—and once again glued myself to the TV screen, watching the story turning from "bad" to "worse", sharing the pains and agony of my American friends, absorbed in my own reflections about our mad and sadly divided world.

I know that America is by for the most powerful nation in the world and could retaliate at very prompt notice—but this was not Pearl Harbor and the enemy was invisible.

In no time, the finger was being pointed at Osama bin Laden and his terrorist group, which had allegedly been behind the previous attack on the World Trade Center and attacks on the American embassies in Nairobi and Dar-Es-Salaam. Bin Laden was supposed to be hiding in a cave somewhere in the mountains of Afghanistan under the patronage of the Taliban. Ironically enough, in the photo I had seen of him, the man looks more like a biblical figure than a hard-headed terrorist leader. Yet according to British intelligence, he is the mastermind behind the Al Quaida network, which is linked to a web of Islamic fundamentalist groups which run operations around the world—including training camps, warehouses, communication, and commercial operations—including the exploitation of the drug trade!

President Bush was starting to speak about "revenge" and the need to catch Osama bin Laden—"dead or alive." I started wondering whether perhaps it would not be best that Bin Laden was never ever caught. Catch him, before you put him in jail or execute him, would he not have to be tried in an open court with CNN beaming his trial across the globe? Would he not become a martyr in the eyes and heart of those who have been taught to hate America?

President Bush has referred to the suicide pilots as "cowards," yet we cannot overlook the fact that these people are, on the other hand, being regarded as martyrs and heroes of "their cause," however misguided they may have been.

That evening I decided to e-mail messages of sympathy to some of my friends in the United States.

In no time, one of them, Patrick Reynolds of Los Angeles, a son of R.J. Reynolds of the U.S. tobacco industry, who, today, ironically heads a nationwide anti-smoking campaign, had acknowledged my message. He said that he was spearheading an initiative for all friends of America, wherever they may be, to light a candle to show that we stand united together, that we will not tolerate terrorism.

That evening I decided to demonstrate my own goodwill towards the American people by working with my staff, late into the night, sending an e-mail message to hundreds of friends all over the world.

The message read:

> Tomorrow Friday night at 7:00 in the evening, wherever you are, step outside and light a candle. We will show the world we stand in solidarity with and support the Americans. We will show the world that people in all nations stand united together against terrorism. Please pass this message to everyone on your

e-mail list. Get your candles ready. We need the world to see.

The next morning when my Secretary accessed my e-mail, we could not just believe the reaction. It was incredible how fast people from all over the world had reacted. On the whole, I was glad that the great majority of messages I received, displayed a great love and solidarity for the American people—but there were also a few thought-provoking reactions.

The first message was from my fifteen-year-old son, Alexander, who is attending College in Brisbane, Australia and was certainly in a confused state of mind:

> Dear Dad—I am absolutely devastated about the attack on New York. Such an act must be considered something beyond malice and revenge. Whoever is responsible for this vicious attack will be brought to justice. I am worried that World War III will start…We have been watching the footage all day and logging on to CNN for the latest news. Whatever happens, one thing is for sure, America will retaliate hard and more lives will be lost. Some footage of Palestinians celebrating after the attack on New York was enough for me. It was like a festival or an early Christmas for them. Do they have no compassion, or can't they accept that this act of terrorism cannot and will not be tolerated by the United States? I don't know, but I remain confused.

This was a spontaneous reaction of an innocent mind, who throughout his young life, has spent an incredible amount of hours viewing CNN. In fact, a few hours after the CNN report, which my son had watched, the BBC was questioning the authenticity of their display of Palestinians in a state of joy after the attacks on America. According to the British media, this footage was about the Palestinians' jubilation following Iraq's invasion of Kuwait some years ago.

One message from Canada quoted some comments by a Canadian television commentator in Toronto:

> This Canadian thinks it is time to speak up for the Americans as the most generous and possibly the least appreciated people on all the Earth. Germany, Japan, and to a lesser extent, Britain and Italy were lifted out of the debris of war by the Americans

who poured in billions of dollars....

Another message quoted an article by Leonard Pitts, Jr., writing in the *Miami Herald*:

> We will go forward from this moment. It is my job to have something to say. They pay me to provide words that help make sense of that, which troubles the American souls. But in this moment of airless shocks when hot tears sting disbelieving eyes, the only thing you can find to say, the only words that seem to fit must be addressed to the unknown author of this suffering. You monster, you beast, you unspeakable bastard. What lesson did you hope to teach us by your cowardly attack on our World Trade Center, our Pentagon, on us? What was it you hoped we would learn...?

Somehow I could understand the deep anger of Mr. Pitts as I looked at images of the devastations in New York and the smoke over the Pentagon.

Another message came from Mr. Raymond St. Ange, a member of Republicans Abroad International who lives and work in Seychelles. St. Ange quoted a message he had received from Joan Shepherd, chairman of their organization:

> My Fellow Americans: I can only imagine your feelings of helplessness upon hearing the news of the diabolical terrorist attacks on American soil—on our homeland. It must be extremely frustrating to be so far from home. My thoughts and prayers are with each and every one of you as they are with all Americans, whether at home or abroad. Please have faith in God and pray for His love and guidance in these extraordinary troubled times...in the face of those devastating attacks on our East Coast, the spirit of solidarity and resolve of Americans across the nation are miraculous to behold. American flags are displayed everywhere, groups of strangers hold candlelight vigils on street corners, and churches and synagogues remain open round-the-clock for prayer. This past weekend, houses of worship across the nation were overflowing; the outpouring of messages and offers of assistance is astounding...

There was no doubt that America was not only in a state of shock but also in a reflective mood.

From New York, Mr. Nichol Gabriel, head of the Joint Office for Commonwealth Permanent Missions to the United Nations, e-mailed to me copy of an editorial from the *New York Times* entitled "National Defense" from which I read:

> Terrorism is a global threat. Part of the challenge for the United States is to recognize that the roots of terrorism lie in economic and political problems in large parts of the world. The end of the Cold War has brought a resurgence of ethnic hatreds that were often stilled by the superpower conflicts between East and West…The United States must, therefore, be adroit as well as strong. It will not be easy to address religious fanaticism or the anger among those left behind by globalization. The distaste of Western civilization and cultural values that fuels terrorism is difficult to overcome.

Then there was this message under the subject reference "All this over a few square miles of land!" It read:

> If Israel had given back the land it took so wrongly, all this could have been avoided. Call your representative in Congress now, and let them know you want us to stop supporting Israel—unless they give back the land they so clearly stole from the Palestinians. There are strong pros and cons to this. The con, of course, is that this would reinforce terrorism, which will never do. But our unquestioning support of the state of Israel will never do either. Israel's immoral actions in the Six Day War precipitated all this, when they stole the land by force. It's time for us to speak up, and let our representatives in congress know how we feel about our nation's unconditional (and immoral) support of Israel. The Israelis could have made peace long ago. So please call your congressperson now, and deliver your feelings. It's time for us to speak up, and take a clear stand on one side or the other. Let us pray for the victims of this terrible tragedy, and for peace. But let's take some real action as well. Thank God we have the freedom to speak up when we believe our government is wrong.

This, of course, reminded me of the ongoing conflict in the Middle East. Cannot the Palestinians and Israelis realize that they are committed by geography alone to live side by side, and that there will be no peace if hate prevails? Was President Bush right to distance United States from the Oslo Peace process after all the efforts President Clinton had displayed during his administration at Camp David and elsewhere?

Another message came supposedly from an art teacher's organization in the United States and was signed "Starla." The message spoke for itself.

> America needs candles for peace not war…Your solidarity must be a resolve for peace on Earth or the United States gets to do what it does best…make war…that is feeding into the Bush regime. Do you not for one minute think like Pearl Harbor, this was allowed to happen? Unite for peace…Anger, war, hatred just keep that mind-set going perpetual—Starla

Then there were the thoughts and questions from Deepak Chopra—who is regarded in the United States as a specialist in the field of spiritual enlightenment.

> All this hatred and anguish seems to have religion at its basis. Isn't something terribly wrong when jihads and wars develop in the name of God? Isn't God invoked with hatred in Ireland, Sri Lanka, India, Pakistan, Israel, Palestine, and even among the intolerant sects of America…? None of us will feel safe again behind the shield of military might and stockpiled arsenals. There can be no safety until the root cause is faced. In this moment of shock, I don't think anyone of us has the answers. It is imperative that we pray and offer solace and help to each other. But if you and I are having a single thought of violence or hatred against anyone in the world at this moment, we are contributing to the wounding of the world.

Perhaps the most comforting and sensible message was the one entitled "Another idea—bomb them with butter."

> Bomb them with butter, bribe them with hope. Last night on NBC it was reported that 81 percent of Americans want restraint. Perhaps this suggestion is what they have been waiting for! A military response, particularly an attack on Afghanistan, is exactly what the terrorists want. It will strengthen and swell their small but fanatical ranks. Instead, bomb Afghanistan with butter, with rice, bread, clothing, and medicine. It will cost less than conventional arms, poses no threat of U.S. casualties, and

just might get the populace thinking that maybe the Taliban does't have the answers. After three years of drought, and with starvation looming, let's offer the Afghani people the vision of a new future. One that includes full stomachs. Bomb them with information. Video players and cassettes of world leaders, particularly Islamic leaders, condemning terrorism. Carpet the country with magazines and newspapers showing the horror of terrorism committed by their 'guest'. Blitz them with laptop computers and DVD players filled with a perspective that is denied them by their government. Saturation bombing with hope will mean that some of it gets through. Send so much that the Taliban can't collect and hide it all.

The Taliban is telling their people to prepare for jihad. Instead, let's give the Afghani people their first good meal in years. Seeing your family fully fed, and the prospect of stability in terms of food and a future is a powerful deterrent to martyrdom. All we ask in return is that they, as a people, agree to enter the civilized world. That includes handing over terrorists in their midst. In responding to terrorism, we need to do something different. Something unexpected, something that addresses the root of the problem. We need to take away the well of despair, ignorance and brutality from which the Osama bin Ladens of the world water their gardens of terror.

Most of the messages were short, thanking me for my thoughts and support at this dreadful time—with most people confirming that they will indeed light a candle to demonstrate their solidarity with the American people. But there were indeed a few exceptions, like this one from Killarney, County Kerry, Ireland:

Hi there…Just a note of your candle-light vigil. I'll be lighting my Canadian candle for all the innocent Vietnamese, Iraqi, Palestinian, etc. casualties that were killed at the hands of American missiles, guns, and other instruments of their military prowess. I don't care if it's 10 or 10,000 people that die, and I'm sure their loved ones don't either. It's a tragedy just the same. Time for America to rethink their foreign policies as well as the motivation for them. There are victims all over the world, man… not just in the states. Peace…

American foreign policy? Over the years I have personally become extremely disenchanted with the way Washington, D.C. had handled and is handling U.S. foreign policy. In fact, in December 1998 I published a book in Seychelles entitled *Oh, Mighty America: the story of David questioning Goliath's behaviour.* Was this not a frank and honest story of a friend of the United States who had become disenchanted with the way Washington, D.C. had handled and was handling U.S. foreign policy?

Suddenly I was reminded once again of Caroline's lamentations "Daddy, Daddy what is becoming of our beautiful America? Who are those people who hate us so much as to wish so much destruction on us at the expense of their own lives?"

A superpower like the United States must be ready to reflect, analyze, and be self-critical. It is certainly not fair play to suggest that you are either on our side or against us. This is playing to the tune of Bin Laden when he says that you are either a believer or an infidel.

# CHAPTER TWO

# OH, MIGHTY AMERICA

OH, MIGHTY AMERICA—believe me for my honor and have respect for my honor in order that you may believe. As a man, I have always cherished the American dreams and ideals. Despite everything, life has been relatively good to me. As a matter of fact, I do believe that I have received more than I deserve of my share of privileges, opportunities, and wealth.

I also once tasted power. I was the founding president of the Republic of Seychelles—a tiny republic, if you want, but also one of the most beautiful countries in the world. Unfortunately, we also became "strategic territory."

Over the years, I have sadly become disenchanted with U.S. foreign policy. I can claim to know something about the subject because for most of my life, I have been greatly affected by it, and its obvious sphere of influence.

In the early sixties, I stuck my neck out when the U.S. airforce decided that it would be in the United States national interest to build a satellite tracking station atop our main island of Mahé to gather military intelligence over a then aggressive Soviet Union. As a young lawyer, I was retained by Philco-Ford Corporation, then based in Palo Alto, California; by Panam Corporation, based in Cape Canaveral, which later became Cape Kennedy, in Florida, and Radio Corporation of America, based in Houston, Texas, to look after their "legal interests".

These three major American corporations had been contracted to front for the U.S. Airforce to build a sophisticated communication and spy station as part of a silent conspiracy between the United States and the United Kingdom in order that the West retain a vital presence in an ocean of growing strategic importance.

Those days, wherever the Americans went, the Soviets were never far behind and, thus, as a budding politician, I soon found myself being branded an "imperial lackey" as I defended the right of the United States to have a presence in the Western Indian Ocean and actively countered the arguments of those who had been briefed by the Soviet Communists to oppose it.

Thus, when the Seychelles tracking station was completed within the stipulated time framework, the government of the United States of America went out of its way to recognize my personal contribution to their vital project and invited me to be their special guest for a two-month tour of their country. It was my first visit to this great country. I was feasted on my arrival in Washington, D.C. by none other than the late Senator John Tower of Texas (who was then chairman of the Senate Armed Services Committee) before I embarked on the start of a "discover the United States itinerary" which enabled me to visit the country as far east as Puerto Rico and as far west as the state of Hawaii.

When, one evening, in a bar in San Francisco, an American fellow turned to me and casually asked, "Buddy, which State are you from?" I realized that if I had told him I came from New York or from New Mexico, he would have accepted this as correct. There and then, I reflected that if ever I was to embrace British or French nationality, I could never truly feel either British or French, but things were certainly different in the land of "hope and glory."

As expected, during that visit to the United States, I was particularly well looked after. I stayed in the best hotels; met a lot of lovely, hospitable and god-fearing people; was handed the gold key of Dade County in Florida and made an honorary citizen of New Orleans—the capital of the state of Louisiana on the August 18, 1965—only seven days after the celebration of my twenty-sixth birthday. At that time, Bill Clinton was only nineteen years old.

I returned to Seychelles ever more converted to the U.S. cause against the spread of international Communism and more than ever committed to support the decision that the United States should establish a presence in the Indian Ocean.

On Monday, July 27, 1998, I found myself under a grapevine in the little town of Andraitx on the Spanish island of Mallorca, Spain, where I came for a Mediterranean holiday. A few days before, I had participated in a conference in the middle of Africa, in Arusha, Tanzania entitled "Leadership Challenges for the Demilitarisation of Africa." As I think and reflect over the speech I had delivered at that conference, I could not help recognizing its anti-American contents and flavor. This did not make me particularly happy.

The morning's headline of the *Daily Bulletin* of Mallorca proclaimed,

### New Aircraft Carrier Commissioned

With guns booming, jets shrieking overhead and President Clinton standing by, the U.S. Navy on Saturday put into service a nuclear-powered aircraft carrier described as the most formidable "man-of-war ever put to sea."

Here under the Spanish sky, on this laid back island of Mallorca, which is often visited by U.S. nuclear-powered naval vessels, I found myself thinking and reflecting. I have families and several good friends in the United States. In a world which has become a global village, the United States today constitutes the only superpower, but has the United States the resolve, the strength, and determination expected of her in order to sustain the role of moral leadership? I was frightened with what I saw on the horizon—a policy of isolation and of greed, a policy which seems to suggest that might will always prove right.

I was born a lively optimist and would hate dying a wretched pessimist. In the aftermath of the dreadful events of September 11, 2001, I believe I have a duty to tell my story. If you are interested about the points I want to make, please read on.

# CHAPTER THREE

# GOD BLESS AMERICA

IN 1962, I QUALIFIED AS A LAWYER IN LONDON and was ready to return home to the Seychelles, then a British colony. The winds of change, which heralded the breaking down of the British Empire was blowing all over the world with the full support and encouragement of the United States and the Soviet Union, which had emerged as the major players in the Cold War game, with China on the sideline determined to establish its own sphere of influence.

There was no airport linking the Seychelles with the outside world at that time. The choice before any traveller to the islands was either to access them by flying to Mombasa in Kenya or Bombay in India and avail of the monthly sailing of a ship of the British India Navigation Company, which plied between the two ports, and on the way called at Port Victoria on our main island of Mahé.

Eager as I have always been to discover as much of the world as possible, I decided that I should catch the ship from Bombay and on the way visit as many metropolis as possible. Thus, I bought a ticket with stopovers in Geneva, Rome, Athens, Istanbul, and Teheran before getting to Bombay.

My 3-day stopover in Istanbul was particularly memorable. I was walking down one of the main thoroughfares of that great city where East meets West (or vice versa), when I found myself facing a huge crowd of colorfully dressed men and women, all extremely agitated. I noticed that they were all facing the Istanbul

Hilton Hotel, and as I got nearer to them, I could make out that they were crying out at the top of their voices "Kennedy, Kennedy! Long live President Kennedy!" in their own peculiar alien accent. I decided to get as close to the front line as possible.

I learnt that these people were refugees who had been pushed into Turkey through Soviet aggression and expansionism. I also learned that the vice president of the United States, Lyndon B. Johnson, was in residence at the Hilton and that the crowd which had gathered had sent a petition to him addressed to President John F. Kennedy, commending his foreign policy generally and his stand against Soviet expansionism in particular.

The crowd had delivered their petition early in the morning and Vice President Johnson had agreed to make an appearance before his departure to Ankara for a NATO meeting, which he was chairing at 11 A.M. I looked at my watch, and it was 10:30 A.M. I looked up again and could feel a sense of commotion in the air. Something was certainly happening. Coming my way was a contingent of American security personnel all courting a lapel bearing the official seal of the United States of America, which identified them as official members of the party of the vice president of the United States.

More and more security people, including a Turkish contingent, surrounded the spot where a loudspeaker had been mounted—not too far from where I had succeeded to penetrate. And, suddenly, somebody made his way to the microphone:"Ladies and Gentlemen, May I introduce to you the Representative of the Vice President of the United States of America, Mr. Carl Rowan."

And there stood in front of me, among the crowd, a distinguished looking black man, overflowing with confidence, surrounded by fellow American bureaucrats of all color, types, and sizes.

People of Azerbaijan, ladies, and gentlemen,

On behalf of the president of the United States of America;
On behalf of Vice President Johnson, who is at the moment taking last-minute instructions from Washington, D.C. before

our imminent departure for Ankara; and on my own personal behalf, I want, first of all, to acknowledge receipt of the petition which you have delivered this morning. Our government has taken due note of your plight and sufferings, which fully confirm the statement which the White House delivered yesterday, deploring the ongoing state of affairs within your native land.

People of Azerbaijan, let me inform you that as long as you, like the people of Turkey, provide us with the moral support which we deem necessary, the forces of aggression will not prevail—and finally, let me take this opportunity to make it clear to one and all that any aggression directed against the soil of the Republic of Turkey will be deemed aggression against the soil of the United States herself.

Perhaps, these were not the exact words of Mr. Carl Rowan, but it was the gist of his address which sunk deep into my memory and made an unforgettable impression. As the translator moved towards the microphone, a proud Mr. Rowan moved one step on the sideline, projecting an image of power, pride, and total faith in the commitments he had just made on behalf of his mighty nation. Again, there were tears in my eyes. I was emotionally overtaken by the United States stand against the spread of international Communism. This event perhaps, more than anything else, decided on which side I was going to be in the ongoing Cold War, which, at that time, was showing a lot of signs of blowing hot.

After the translation was over, there was a sense of high jubilation among the crowd. A little girl was ushered in to deliver a bouquet of red roses—destined for President Kennedy. As the crowd shouted "Kennedy! Kennedy! Long live President Kennedy!" I had my last glance at Carl Rowan.[1] He looked contented, smart, and efficient and once again, I said to myself, "God Bless America."

Against the background of the terrorist war on America, it is

---

[1]Carl Rowan was born in 1952. He was Deputy Assistant Secretary of State for Public Affairs between 1961 and 1963, Ambassador to Finland from 1963 to 1964 and Director of the U.S. Information Agency between 1964 and 1965. Afterwards, he became a nationwide syndicated columnist.

pertinent to realize that all these jubilantly pro-United States refu-gees from Azerbaijan were of the Muslim faith. How fast can people change! But then it is pertinent to remember that despite Pearl Harbor and Hiroshima, the United States and Japan entertain to-day an important and active military pact in the Pacific.

# CHAPTER FOUR

# TENSION ON THE HORIZON

WHEN I GOT BACK TO SEYCHELLES, I found out that although there was increasing concern among the Seychellois about the British government's policy of dismantling the empire, the islands, nonetheless, constituted an oasis of friendliness, peace, and stability in an otherwise troublesome world. This atmosphere had justified visitors from overseas referring to us as "The Last Lost Paradise." No Seychellois at that time, of course, had ever realised that their 110 islands, which are spread over nearly a million square miles of the western Indian Ocean, south of the oil-producing nations of the Middle East and the Gulf, constituted strategic territory, and that while the Seychellois were going about their daily lives with a smile on their face and *joie de vivre* in their heart, Washington, D.C. and London were locked up in a silent conspiracy about their future.

Soon afterwards, political tension started mounting in the islands when the Seychelles Tax Payers and Producers Association (a group made up of the ruling elite of merchants and landowners) started talking about a unilateral declaration of independence in the manner Ian Smith had proceeded in Southern Rhodesia (now Zimbabwe) against international public opinion.

Tension, of course, was also being heightened by the start of a debate in London as to whether the time had not come for Britain to pull out east of Suez and to get the Americans to fill the vacuum they would leave behind.

The Suez Canal was built in 1869 under the leadership of the

French promoter, Ferdinand de Lesseps. Upon its completion, the British, having recognized its vast strategic and economic importance to the growing empire, acquired substantial interest in the enterprise. They had found that two weeks of rugged sailing around Africa's Cape of Good Hope could be eliminated for shipment, between England and her Asian colonies.

Over several decades, the United Kingdom stationed British troops along the canal zone and in several countries east of Suez. However, with the rise of nationalist fervor in Egypt, British troops left the canal zone in June 1956. In July of that same year, the United States and Great Britain withdrew offers to help finance the Aswan High Dam across the Nile River. This and other factors led to the take over of the canal by Egyptian president Gamal A. Nasser on July 26, 1956, when he announced that Egypt would use the canal tolls to build the dam. Western nations simply protested the action but Israel, long upset over the canal's politics, on October 29, 1956 made a prolonged attack against Egypt. By October 31, Great Britain and France were drawn into the fight. On November 5, Anglo-French troops landed near Port Said. Egypt's Arab neighbors did not come to its aid, but the USSR threatened to retaliate with nuclear weapons. The United States, working through the United Nations, demanded a cease-fire. One was put into effect on November 6, and a supervisory police force established by the United Nations took over on March 7, 1957, when the canal was re-opened under Egyptian control.

In fact, I was on board the S.S. *Braemar Castle* of the Union Castle Line, when she was the first ship to pass through the canal after the Israel and Anglo-French invasion. I was a passenger on this ship, a young and innocent islander on my way to London to study law, and now Britain had not only decided to dismantle its vast Empire but was also contemplating pulling out east of Suez. What domino effect would such a decision have on the future of our scattered group of islands in the wilderness of the Indian Ocean?

When a few months later, a by-election was announced to fill the vacancy for the legislative seat of our small capital, Victoria, I decided I had enough energy to combine law and politics. I stood as a candidate and won the seat with a great majority, and under my leadership was born a political movement which later took the name of the Seychelles Democratic Party.

On the morning, I had returned to Port Victoria by slow boat, the Island of Mahé was standing in clear relief over the glorious background created by the rising sun. That moment, I realized that while most Europeans were living in a "black, white, and grey" atmosphere for at least six months of the year, we, in Seychelles were living in technicolor throughout the year. I also realized that with an international airport, we could become a 5-star tourism destination. It was, therefore, not surprising that as an elected member of our legislative council, my first priority was to have an airport built which would enable us to break away from the isolation which had characterized our past.

But, we relied on a coconut economy. The islands had no money for such an infrastructure, however essential. At first the idea received nothing but a cool reception from the British government. One day, however, I was invited to London to be told the good news! The United Kingdom had decided to finance an airport for us but not just any airport. We were to have the latest "state-of-the-art" airport big enough to land jumbo jets. Later, I realized that one vital condition was that the airport could also be used for Western military purposes—if ever required.

# CHAPTER FIVE

# THE U.S. TRACKING STATION

A FEW MONTHS FOLLOWING MY ELECTION to the Seychelles legislative council, a yacht flying the flag of the United States of America arrived in Port Victoria. *Wanderlure* was captained by its owner, Carl Heintz of Santa Barbara, California. A few days later, I received an invitation from Carl and Eleonore Heintz to dine with them on their sumptuous vessel. Compared to the British who were normally cool and reserved, the Heintzs were generous and exuberant in their disposition as they hosted me to a lunch of Caesar salad and prime New York steak along with a good Napa Valley wine carrying a Robert Mondavi label. I think it was a Cabernet-Sauvignon…

I saw a lot of the Heintzs during their two-week stopover in Seychelles and grew to like them enormously. On the last evening, Carl Heintz said that he wanted to tell me something on a very confidential basis. The United States was interested in building a communication project in the Seychelles—something of great importance. He said that some people were expected in Mahé soon and would call on me.

I was, therefore, not surprised when a few months later, I found myself facing three high-powered gentlemen all formally attired in suits and ties. I cannot remember their exact names but each one of them was senior vice president of a major U.S. corporation, namely Philco-Ford, Pan-American, and Radio Corporation of America. They said that their companies had entered into a contract with the U.S. government to build a modern U.S. satellite tracking station for and on behalf of the United States airforce. However, they made it clear that all emphasis should be placed on the civilian aspect of the project and that the airforce connection was to be played down to the lowest possible level. They had received recommendation to retain me as their lawyer to look after their companies' legal interests.

I was, of course, flattered by the offer and suddenly felt secure in the knowledge that each month I was to collect a retainer fee plus acceptable, reasonable expenses. Indeed, the few hundred dollars I received each month from these companies were "peanuts" in New York legal costs framework. In the Seychelles of that time, it constituted a substantial contribution to my monthly income, and I was happy.

I was, of course, always eager to find out why of all places in the world, the United States had chosen to build a satellite tracking station in Seychelles. Following the announcement of the project, there were all sorts of speculation as to the true purpose of the station and, indeed, a lot of negative allegations from the Soviet camp.

I was privileged on Wednesday, August 31, 1963, to attend a lecture by Colonel E.E. Lasch who was the first United States airforce officer in charge of the Seychelles station. Colonel Lasch was a man of impressive stature and was often smoking from a huge pipe, which seemed to have been chosen to match his physical size.

First, Colonel Lasch pointed out that there were several networks of satellite tracking stations throughout the world, as well as several separate networks within the United States. One of these networks was NASA, which he described as the national network primarily concerned with the U.S. "man-in-space" flights. He said there was another United States network, which was engaged in research projects aimed at finding out conditions in space such as temperature change and all the scientific data which was needed to ensure proper operation of all types of vehicles in space. He said that the station in Seychelles belonged to the research and development network operated by civilians under contract to the United

States airforce with its main control centre at Sunnyvale, California. The satellite control station in Seychelles would send information via satellites to the center in Sunnyvale. Now, why did the United States want to set up a station in the Seychelles? Colonel Lasch explained that the main reason was its location:

> If you look at the globe of the Earth and go halfway round the globe from Sunnyvale, California, you will see that the Seychelles are situated nearly opposite to Sunnyvale. Mahé is either 179 degrees or 181 of longitude from Sunnyvale, depending upon which direction, east or west, you have taken. Secondly, we wanted a site very close to the equator. As the Seychelles fill these two requirements, that is the reason why we are here.

Unfortunately, in those days, wherever the Americans went, the Soviets were not far behind, and in no time, I found myself branded an "imperial lackey" for defending the Americans' arrival on our shores. In no time, too, the Soviets had provoked the emergence of an active anti-American nucleus in the politics of the islands. Soon enough, the Seychelles Democratic Party, which I had started found itself in a confrontational position vis-à-vis the Soviet, backed and inspired Seychelles People's United Party (the SPUP), led by another charismatic lawyer, Mr. France A. René. From the start, the SPUP opposed the United States presence and called for outright independence from Great Britain.

For the first time in its history, the Seychellois people found themselves divided into two camps—the *Blue* and the *Red,* those for the U.S. presence and those against it. One evening, SPUP activists would paint slogans in strategic positions all over Mahé calling "Yankees to go home!" The next day, the islanders would wake up to discover that all the "Yankees, go home" slogans had been removed and replaced by new ones proclaiming in big blue letters, "Yankee, Yes—Communism, No!" I was proud to be the mastermind behind the pro-U.S. stands.

It took me several years to realize that Colonel Lasch had not really told us, in his lecture, everything about this famous airforce station. Years later, it took a CBS's *60 Minutes* documentary to inform me that it was, indeed, a station to gather military intelligence over the Soviet Union and other nations. This information was confirmed when an article in the U.S. airforce magazine. *Orbiter,* revealed that:

"The mission of the Seychelles station was to operate and maintain a remote tracking station to launch critical first acquisition and on-orbit command and control of more than 90 satellites supporting the war-fighting nations of all unified and specified commands. The station also provides direct support to the space shuttle and to NASA, NATO, and allied nations' satellites. It operates a defence satellite communications system terminal and performs total small base support. The station, located five miles south of Victoria, has been part of the US. airforce tracking network since 1963. 'Indi'—as the station is often called—handles more than 10,000 operation supports each year."

The *Orbiter* article was published in the aftermath of the Gulf War.

Looking back over the years, I must in all sincerity, admit that the decision of the United States to establish a presence in our islands marked the beginning of the end of the period known as *"La belle époque"*—that wonderful innocent era of sweet and peaceful life which had earned the Seychelles the reputation of being "The Last Lost Paradise" and the Seychellois, the reputation of being "among the friendliest people in the world."

What I also eventually came to realize was that had there been a war between the United States and the Soviet Union, our small island of Mahé with its U.S. tracking station protruding from one of its mountain peaks like a huge golf ball for all to see, would have been a prime target for destruction. And like the two towers of the World Trade Center in New York City, Mahé could have abruptly gone up in flames!

# CHAPTER SIX

# COLD WAR BRINGS CLOUDS OVER PARADISE

DURING THE CONSTRUCTION OF THE TRACKING STATION, several hundred people from the United States and elsewhere came to Seychelles to work. Once the station became operational, there were some 150 to 200 U.S. nationals besides 200 or more Seychellois employed to service it. As the lawyer retained to look after the legal interest of the three major companies involved in the construction, maintenance, and operation of the station, I established regular contact at both professional and social levels with our new American residents.

My first impression was that the U.S. citizens who had come from the West Coast were more easygoing and more easily adaptable to a multiracial ambience than those who had come from the East Coast, who were on average, more conservative in their outlook. Secondly, I was expecting most of these so-called "electronic experts" to have a broader academic background than was the case. I guess that if you had become an electronic expert at the age of twenty-five, this must have been through a process of specialization, and at the expense of other subjects like history, geography, scripture, and literature, which those of us educated in the Seychelles by missionaries, had always taken to heart.

Nonetheless, the Americans who descended on our shores with their greenbacks and U.S. passports, their sports car, and their Hilton Hotel, type accommodation on top of the hill were an

overnight hit with our women. In no time, we were having a social problem to counter with. The Americans had, more or less,
monopolized all the beautiful ladies, with an increasing number
of broken-hearted Seychellois boyfriends and husbands wondering what would happen next.

These problems converged on my desk on a daily basis. There
was nothing illegal about these liaisons, which went hand in hand
with the creolization process prevailing in Seychelles, except that
it was all going in one direction. The American men were getting
involved with local ladies, but there were no American ladies to
provide a counter-balance.

Every now and then, one American would die either of a mo-
torcycle or a motor car accident, and then I had to organize the
legal clearance to get the body home to the United States via
Mombasa, Nairobi, or London to the U.S. destination. It was a
long and costly affair. It made me think about the Vietnam War—
the first war where one of the warring nations was wealthy enough
to seek the bodies of its fallen soldiers and transport them back
home for a dignified burial. But at what emotional and other costs
to the nation, the family of the dead soldier, and to the army itself? In a democratic society, the arrival of each dead body created
a moment for reflection, a debate as to whether "our children"
should be on the battlefield at all. The enemies, of course, took
note of the growing division within the nation and became aware
that the resolve to continue the war was on the wane, notwithstanding what the commander in chief in the White House and
the generals on the field were saying.

My task as a consultant and legal adviser was, however, made
easier by a ruling emanating from the U.S. government that during the construction stage of the station, any U.S. citizens who
got involved in a conflict or dispute with a Seychellois would be
sent back to the United States promptly without any recourse to
adjudication. The tracking station had to be completed in record
time, and it was in the national interest that construction took
place in an atmosphere of as little local controversy as possible. In
this respect, U.S. airforce discipline was made to override the demo-

cratic right of the individual. But if such was the U.S. government's attitude in its endeavor to promote and cultivate the best possible relationship with the locals, those who had started to act on behalf of the Soviets were not to be appeased. Instead, they vigorously initiated a proactive "Hate the Americans"campaign within the islands.

One day, they denounced the Americans for utilizing their purchasing power to buy all the lobsters on the local market. When the Americans decided to stop buying local lobsters and to import their requirements from South Africa, they were criticized as supportive of the apartheid regime and acting in a manner prejudicial to the well-being of the local fishermen. It was obviously a hard case for the Americans to win—and here, I was, contributing my share as a professional, to the fight against scientific Socialism, which was then seen as committed to impose Communism on the international community. At least, this was the message the *Voice of America* was busily echoing in the four corners of the globe, and I fully believed in it.

While from a political standpoint, I was able to point out that the setting up of the tracking station in Seychelles brought great economic benefit to the country, and would help put us on the international map, when the agreement entered into between the government of the United Kingdom and the government of the United States was published, several provisos in it provided ammunition to those who were politically committed against it.

Under this agreement, for example, (i) access to the site was not granted to persons not officially connected with the facilities except with the consent of the representatives designated for that purpose by the United States government or the government of the United Kingdom; (ii) title to any removable property imported or procured in Seychelles by the United States government, or a United States contractor, shall remain in the United States Government. Such property including official papers, shall be exempt from inspection, search and seizure; (iii) military members of the United States forces who may be brought into Seychelles for the purposes of this agreement shall be exempt from passport and visa requirements, immigration inspection, and any registration or control as aliens; (iv) no import, excise, consumption, or other tax duty or impost shall be charged on material, equipment, supplies, or goods for use in the establishment, maintenance, or operation of the facilities which are consigned or destined for the United States authorities or a United States contractor; (v) no tax or fee shall be payable in respect of registration or licensing for use in Seychelles of motor vehicles belonging to the United States government or United States contractors; (vi) no member of the United States forces or nationals of the United States serving or employed in Seychelles in connection with the establishment, maintenance, or operation of the facilities with which this agreement is concerned, and residing in Seychelles, has reason to pay income tax in Seychelles, except with respect to income derived from Seychelles.

There was also a long paragraph on criminal jurisdiction which went a long way to make it difficult for a Seychelles court to exercise jurisdiction over a U.S. national employed at the station. And to make matters worse, while the government of the United Kingdom was supposed to have consulted with the government of Seychelles in the matter, the government of Seychelles was not a party to the agreement.

It was certainly not an easy package to sell, but with charm and local goodwill, I did my share to countenance the attitude and action of the anti-American nucleus.

# CHAPTER SEVEN

# KENNEDY'S GLOBAL IMPACT

ON NOVEMBER 22, 1963 PRESIDENT KENNEDY and the first lady arrived at Love Field in Dallas, Texas. The presidential motorcade then departed for a trip downtown where the president was scheduled to speak at a meeting of the citizens' council. The president and the first lady were riding in an open-top limousine accompanied by Texas governor, John B. Connolly and his wife. At 12:30 P.M. on Elm Street, in downtown Texas, the motorcade was slowly approaching a triple underpass. Shots rang out, the president was struck in the back, then in the head and was mortally wounded. At Parkland Memorial Hospital, the president's limousine remained outside the emergency room where some 15 doctors tried in vain to save him. At 1 P.M., John Fitzgerald Kennedy was pronounced dead.

On that day, I was on the S.S. *Karanja,* halfway between Seychelles and the Port of Mombasa in Kenya in a time zone which is around nine hours ahead of Texas. We heard about President Kennedy's assassination on the BBC *World Service* when we woke up the next day for breakfast. No one, today, would believe the impact which this news had on the S.S. *Karanja* that morning. British officers; Goanese stewards; the Chinese who ran the laundry and dry-cleaning department; Christians; Muslims; Hindus; Bhudists; and Bahais were all literally in tears, as if the world had suddenly stopped moving.

No one could imagine the extent of the impact which the Kennedy presidency had made globally in so short a time. In fact,

John F. Kennedy had surrounded himself with the most efficient PR team ever assembled since Coca-Cola, with the result that when his assassination was announced, there was an instant deep sense of anger, loss, and agitation within the international community. The United States had suddenly lost its 35th president. The world had lost the man they had been made to love and respect—a world leader who symbolized hope for a better and more just tomorrow. At least, this was the sentiment prevailing on board the S.S. *Karanja* on that sad morning.

As a student of history, I had learned about Francis Key writing the *Star Spangled Banner* whilst being held on the Royal Navy frigate during the British attack on Fort Mettering in the War of 1812. Alone on the far back of the deck of the *Karanja,* faced with a featureless horizon, I paid my own tribute to the man who had inspired me to enter politics by recalling to mind some of the inspiring words of the national anthem of his great nation:

> *Oh, say, can you see*
> *By the dawn's early light*
> *What so proudly we hailed*
> *At the twilight's last gleaming?*
> *Whose broad stripes and bright stars*
> *Through the perilous fight.*
> *O'er the ramparts we watched*
> *Were so galantly streaming?*
> *And the rockets' red glare*
> *The bombs bursting in air*
> *Gave proof through the night*
> *That our flag was still there.*
> *Oh, say, does the star-spangled banner yet wave*
> *O'er the land of the free*
> *And the home of the brave?*

# CHAPTER EIGHT

# IN AWE OF AMERICA

As a result of my role in Seychelles in support of the build-up of the tracking station, I was to receive an invitation to visit the United States as a guest of the U.S. government.

I was accorded a VIP welcome when I landed at Washington National Airport on a flight from London in July 1965. The first item on my program was a courtesy call at the State Department on Secretary of State Mennen G. Williams who had been governor of the state of Michigan for several years before being made Secretary of State for African Affairs by President Kennedy. I had been introduced to Governor Williams some months before at the New Stanley Hotel in Nairobi when he was leading the U.S. delegation to Kenya's independence celebrations. At that time, his colleagues referred to him as "Soapy Williams" because he was associated with Mennen Cosmetics, which, at one time, was a household name in the United States. Governor Mennen Williams was an impressive figure. I remember watching him on the night of the Independence Day gala, which President Jomo Kenyatta was hosting at State House, Nairobi, sipping one Bloody Mary after another. Some months later, he became especially endeared to the African people when he was slapped by a white farmer on his arrival in Salisbury, Rhodesia (now Harare, Zimbabwe) after he had made a statement in favor of majority rule.

At our meeting, Governor Williams expressed gratitude on the part of his government for my contribution to the build-up, on time, of the tracking station in Seychelles. He said that the invitation for me to visit his country was an acknowledgement of their gratefulness. He explained that while the State Department had organized a program which would take me as far east as Puerto Rico and as far west as Hawaii, if there was any place in the United States I wanted to visit which had been left out, then I should ask and they would oblige. He then introduced me to Everett Waldo, a former minister of the Methodist Church, who was going to accompany me throughout my American visit.

Mr. Waldo later escorted me on a tour of the U.S. Capital, visiting the White House, Congress, the Pentagon, and the other great historic monuments, which provide a special dimension to Washington, D.C.

That evening, I was the guest of honor at a cocktail party at the Washington Hilton, hosted by Senator John Tower of Texas in his capacity as chairman of the Senate Armed Services Committee. John Tower had become the senator from Texas when he was elected to fill the vacancy caused by the election of Lyndon B. Johnson as vice-president of the United States. During the reception, which was attended mostly by representatives of the United States airforce and representatives of the major American corporations contracted to build the tracking station, I remember well Senator Tower and I posing for a special photo against a large map of the western Indian Ocean, with both of us pointing towards the Seychelles to demonstrate the growing strategic importance of our archipelago. At the end of the reception, the senator confided in me about the ongoing talks between his government and the government of the United Kingdom for the establishment of a U.S. base in the Indian Ocean.

The next day, Everett Waldo and I flew to New York City, where we spent five days at the Waldorf Astoria, the luxury hotel which Conrad Hilton had built in Manhattan and which represented my first experience in a five-star plus establishment. Besides a meeting at the African-American Institute, my program in New York included a visit to the United Nations, where I had been scheduled to pay a courtesy call on U Thant, who had succeeded Dag Hammarskjold in 1961 as secretary general of the organization following the mysterious and controversial demise of Hammarskjold in a plane crash while on a mission to the Congo.

Unfortunately, my visit to New York coincided with the passing away of Adlai Stevenson who had since 1961 been his country's ambassador to the United Nations. I had, of course, read a lot about Mr. Stevenson, who had vaulted into national prominence as governor of Illinois, and who had been twice nominated as the Democratic Party's presidential candidate, although losing both elections to General Dwight D. Eisenhower. That day, I felt especially privileged when I received an invitation to attend a memorial service at the United Nations headquarters in honor of Mr. Stevenson. It was there that I shook hands with Secretary General, U Thant, and met the great American poet, Archibald MacLeish, who was known as the "poet laureate of the New Deal" and who, on that occasion, delivered an impressive and emotional eulogy about the greatly respected but sadly departed U.S. statesman.

From New York, we flew to Burlington, Vermont where I was the houseguest of a former Republican state senator whose family descended from the family of Cornelius Vanderbilt, who had built one of the great transnational railway systems. Unfortunately, I cannot recall to mind the name of this hospitable and generous family who made me feel at home at their grand residence overlooking Lake Champlain where I remember experiencing my first freshwater swim. The next day, the visit of a man from the Seychelles to Vermont made news in the *Burlington Free Post*.

From Vermont, we headed eastwards to Puerto Rico. While there, I stayed at the El Convento hotel, which had, once upon a time, been a convent. Of course, the Puerto Rican landscape resembled a lot the landscape of Seychelles, although at that time, I was more interested to see how Puerto Rico's associated statehood status was working with the United States. The residents of this island (which was acquired by the United States some one hundred years ago as spoils from the Spanish-American War) are Americans who do not pay federal income taxes, do not elect members of Congress and cannot vote for president. However, after talking to several Puerto Ricans, I found that this diminished status had the support of many of the islanders who were worried that state-hood would jeopardize their island's distinctive heritage.

From Puerto Rico, it was back to the mainland. In fact, to Tampa, Florida where I had a rendezvous with my old friends, Carl and Eleonor Heinz. They had lost their yacht, *Wanderlure*, on the great barrier reef off Belize in Central America on their way back home. Now, they were supervising the building of *Wanderlure II* in the Everglades, Florida. I stayed several days with the Heinzs, during which time they escorted me to Dade County, where I received the freedom key from Mayor Chuck Hall. As the Heinzs were not going to be at their normal residence in Santa Barbara, California during my coming visit to the West Coast, they had asked their son, Carl Jr., to provide me with a taste of Californian hospitality.

When I got to Los Angeles, Carl Jr. was at the airport to welcome me together with his business partner, Pete Malatesta, the nephew of Bob Hope. Thus was the door of Hollywood and those who socially patronized it open to me for the days that I was there. I found Los Angeles itself, as a city, somewhat monotonous from an architectural standpoint, but Beverley Hills and Bel Air areas were certainly different, with beautiful villas standing in lush tropi-cal gardens of exotic flowers and private walkways and swimming pools. Carl Heintz Jr. introduced me to many prominent people living there.

There were three items of special interest earmarked under the Los Angeles itinerary. There was, first, a visit to Disney World amusement park and then a visit to Palm Springs, which is a desert city about 160 miles from Los Angeles in Riverside County sub-urb, California. I was going there to meet with an old penpal, Mr. Robert Spinks, who was trying to grow a coco-de-mer palm in this fashionable resort. (The coco-de-mer is a unique palm which only grows in Seychelles.) As a member of a philatelist club, I was only fifteen years old when I received a letter from none other than the famous Walt Disney requesting that I put on board a Japanese fishing vessel, which was in the harbor at Port Victoria, a few germinating coco-de-mer seeds. These nuts were consigned to

Mr. Disney, care of a certain Mr. Sataki in Hiroshima, Japan. Sataki and Walt Disney were friends, and each one was eager to grow a coco-de-mer palm in their winter garden. Indeed, I recall well the day when I received as a consideration for despatching the coco-de-mer seedlings a collection of Walt Disney films from the RKO theater in Bombay. They had been sent by Mr. Disney. Unfortunately, these films had to be sent back unviewed because at that time, we had no projector in the islands capable of showing them.

The next exciting item was a sailing tour around the island of Santa Catalina. That day, we boarded an up-market yacht at the Balboa Yacht Club in Newport. There was a galaxy of young and beautiful people on board the yacht, which included two children of the arch-conservative governor of Arizona, Barry Goldwater. Without really knowing, I was moving in the circle of some of the staunchest right-wing Republicans in the country. They were a jolly lot, and as we sailed around the island, enjoying chilled wine and good food, we stopped in many spots to dive and swim. We were having a good time until the skipper of the yacht brought to our attention a news item he had just heard over the radio that Watts, a neighborhood in Los Angeles, was exploding. Rioting mobs of angry blacks were breaking into stores and stealing everything. They were setting fire to buildings, yelling, "Burn, baby, burn!" According to the radio, the police were having difficulty stopping them. Some people had been killed, and soldiers had been called in. Suddenly, a wave of fear had swept across the yacht, with everybody looking worried and frightened. It would appear that blacks in this area were sick and tired of waiting for a better life. They were tired of slums, tired of bad jobs and poor pay, and tired of hearing Martin Luther King Jr. asking them to be patient.

It was there and then decided that we return to Newport immediately and make our way back to Los Angeles. Being in the midst of frightened people, I also became frightened and never more than, when on the road to Los Angeles, we drove to a gun shop, where my friends bought guns and revolvers of all sizes—and there I was for the first time, in possession of a deadly weapon, which I hardly knew how to handle. This experience, of course, made me think of the cowboy side of the Americans and reminded me of all those films of Hopalong Cassidy, Gene Autry, Sunset Carson, and Roy Rogers, which I had seen during my college days after someone had opened up a small cinema in Seychelles. It also made me realize how easy it was to buy a gun or a revolver in the United States. By the time I left Los Angeles for San Francisco, several people had been killed in the riot, which must have cost millions of dollars in damages and destruction.

In San Francisco, I stayed at the Fairmont Hotel on Telegraph Hill. It was there while I was having a drink at the revolving bar which overlooks the city of San Francisco and its harbour that I was asked which state I came from. It was also there that I met with my friend, Bill Pomeroy, a distinguished American. Bill was proud to show me the city of his birth, for it is from there that the family operated a major building construction corporation, which made the Pomeroys a relatively wealthy family. They owned an art gallery in downtown San Francisco, which was run by Bill's daughter, Peggy, who was then married to one of the sons of Herbert Hoover, a former President of the United States. Bill took me to Fisherman's Wharf, for a drive along Sausolito and then up to Hilsborough where he lived. His friend, Bing Crosby, was a neighbor. He gave me a taste of the Pacific on the eve of my departure for Hawaii by taking me to dinner at the Traders' Vic Restaurant where I ate Samoan suckling pig and drank a lot of planter's punch.

Nowhere in the United States, did I feel more at home than in Hawaii. I guess I felt close to the warmth exuded by the people who were predominantly Eurasians, Polynesians, Micronesians, and people of Chinese, Japanese, and Caucasian ancestry all living in an intermingled way. The choice of food at the Ala Moana Shopping Center in downtown Honolulu was spicy and to my taste. At the Princess Kauliani Hotel, a Sheraton-run establishment, I remember having breakfast on a patio overlooking Waikki Beach, enjoying half of a pawpaw and a glass of freshly sqeezed guava juice in the company of a couple of minah birds. It was just like home in Seychelles, except somewhat more sophisticated from a Western standpoint. While there, I got romantically involved with a girl from the mainland who was working in the hotel bookshop. It was a wonderful way to culminate a great visit to the United States.

Nostalgia may not be what it used to be, but my stay in Hawaii certainly reminded me of my Boy Scout days in Seychelles when we used to go camping to the outer islands and organized campfires. There was a song we especially sang about Hawaii. It was a farewell song:

> *Good-bye Hawaii*
> *Good-bye that land of paradise*
> *I will keep your memory*
> *To guide me on my way*
> *Islands of dreams,*
> *It is time to depart*
> *Sweet Honolulu,*
> *I will always cry for you.*

Travelling through America, I found it a land of great contrast. The Americans are among the richest people on the globe, yet millions are still poor. The Americans are among the most materialistic people, yet among the most spiritual. The Americans are among the most friendly and generous, but some are still very grasping and violent. Politically, they can be ultra radical and ultra conservative. They come in all colors and in all sizes, from over 7-foot tall volleyball players to small circus dwarves. After, such a wonderful trip with such fond memories, I knew I could fit in the American society and with pride join other Americans in singing:

> *Oh beautiful for spacious skies*
> *For amber waves of grain*
> *For purple mountains majesties*
> *Above the fruited plains*
> *America, America*
> *God shed his grace on thee*
> *And crowned thy good brotherhood*
> *From sea to shining sea.*

# CHAPTER NINE

# ALDABRA—WHERE BIRDS AND TORTOISES REMAIN KING

WHEN I RETURNED TO SEYCHELLES FROM THE UNITED STATES, one of the first persons who wanted to see me urgently was Tony Beamish, an entomologist who had a passionate interest in birds and who travelled extensively, making films about birds and other animals. We had met some months before when he had come to Seychelles to make a research on the black parrots on Praslin, the paradise fly catcher on La Digue, and the magpie robin on Frégate island.

"Jimmy," he asked, "Did the Americans tell you about their plans to build a naval-cum-military base on Aldabra?"

"Aldabra?… No…," I replied, for although Senator John Tower had spoken about ongoing talks between the United States and United Kingdom governments regarding the establishment of a base in the Indian Ocean, there had been no specific mention of Aldabra. Indeed, if Senator Tower had mentioned Aldabra, I would have told him why it was the wrong place to choose.

Aldabra atoll is a natural history museum tucked away in a lost corner of the Indian Ocean, 650 miles from Mahé Island. For man, it is an achievement just to stay alive on Aldabra, but for the tortoises and birds, it is a paradise.

I had visited Aldabra once as a guest of the Swedish-American pioneer of ecotourism, Lars Eric Lindblad from Connecticut on his cruiseship, the *Lindblad Explorer*. We had journeyed around the island's seventy-mile rim of honeycombed coral, so sharp and spiky that it cut our climbing boots to ribbons. Unique animals and birds dwell on the soilless and waterless atoll, such as the 75,000 giant land tortoises, a population far outnumbering the 3,000 that survive in their only other refuge on the Galapagos Islands. The frigate bird with its seven-foot wing span is one of the rarest birds in the world. Several other flightless birds are in this region which at one time included the now extinct Dodo.

Tony Beamish had just returned from making a film on Aldabra, which he was going to use in the biggest conservation battle of all times, in an attempt to stop the plans of the British and American governments to construct an airfield there. In no time, articles with headlines like, "Battle for Survival"—"Flightless Rail against the VC10"—"Airfield Scheme as Threat to Island" were making top news in London newspapers in a campaign to save Aldabra—a campaign which was aggressively supported by the Royal Society for the protection of birds.

There was a lively response from the United States as well. Professor Evelyne Hutchinson, professor of Zoology at Yale University, declared that, "The destruction of wildlife on Aldabra would lead to a paramount gap in our understanding of the living world." The *New York Times* of February 24, 1968 reminded its readers that this was not the first time scientists had rallied to the defence of Aldabra. Charles Darwin himself had done so nearly a hundred years before. The New York newspaper urged conservationists to cheer up and take a broad view of the matter.

"The coming decimation of the atoll!" the leading article said, "is itself a splendid specimen of evolution in action, illustrating as it does, the universal tendency to destroy all forms of life that are less noisy, brutal, and demented than itself."

In the House of Commons, however, the British minister of defence, Mr. Healey, was unable to give any assurance that Aldabra would not be developed. He stated that a decision would be taken within twelve months, that alternative sites had been ruled out for "compelling reasons," and that "Scientific bodies concerned would be consulted if it were decided to go ahead with the defence plans for an airfield and harbor."

As expected, Mr. Healey's comments in the House of Commons was not to be the end of the matter. On August 5, a letter to *The Times* newspaper signed by the heads of the main protection societies in the United Kingdom said that it was not the object to question the need for a staging airfield, although it would be helpful if the government would give its reasons and proceeded to pinpoint the problems and hazards of the scheme:

> The island has no harbor and is composed of coral rocks undermined and dissected by the sea. The plan is to dam the lagoon, which is tidal and the size of the Thames estuary, to make a port and then to build a causeway thirty miles long...even before the construction is complete, the scientific value of the island would have been irreversibly damaged. Then the authorities will have to overcome the problem of bird-aircraft collisions, likely at Aldabra to be the worst in the world...

This letter provoked a lively correspondence in *The Times* column, which lasted for three weeks. One of the letters was from Alistair Buchan of the Institute for Strategic Studies. This questioned, for the first time, the defence strategy that had led to the choice of Aldabra.

After the defence correspondent of *The Times,* Charles Douglas-Home, had questioned the strategic value of an airfield on the atoll, Air Marshall Boyle of the British Ministry of Defence leapt into print. "Aldabra would give us more strategic mobility. It would help to provide a means of access and our own control to the Far East...the need for strategic mobility grows more, not less", he wrote.

From the United States, the journal *Science* carried a letter from the secretary of the Smithsonian Institution, S. Dillon Ripley, saying they were "...deeply concerned over the possibility of military development on the most scientifically interesting atoll in the world."

And a few days later, the *Washington Evening Star* declared that "...nowhere is man's inability to live well alone more vividly illustrated than on Aldabra." Even more significant was the publication of an exchange of letters between the National Wildlife Federation of the United States and the then Secretary for Defence Robert S. McNamara. The federation, "speaking for more than two million persons," expressed concern over the atoll's fate and asked that the Pentagon should use its influence to persuade the British government to select an alternative site for the airfield. In his reply, Mr. McNamara assured the Federation that the "…importance of Aldabra as a scientific laboratory is fully recognized throughout our government. We have notified officially the concern of the U.S. scientific community to the British."

Again, that was not going to be the end of the matter. In the House of Lords in London, a leading conservationist, Lord Ridley announced that he would be seeking a debate at the end of November. Meanwhile, a television documentary filmed by Tony Beamish called *Island in Danger* was broadcast by the BBC on October 29 and was followed by televised debate. Support for the Royal Society's cause became overwhelming among the public, scientific and conservation establishments.

Then, as suddenly as the crisis had blown up, it was over. On November 18, 1967, it was announced that the pound sterling would be devalued and that there would no longer be a British military presence east of Suez. A few days later, on November 22, the British government's decision not to go ahead with their plans for Aldabra was officially confirmed.

Those who are interested in the long saga to save Aldabra should read Tony Beamish's book, *Aldabra Alone,* published in London in 1970 by Allen and Unwin Ltd. with a foreword by the great British biologist, Sir Julian Huxley. It is concluded with the statement: "As a natural treasure house, Aldabra must belong to the whole world. To sacrifice such a legacy for temporary strategic gain would be an act of vandalism."

The United Nations proclaimed Aldabra a world heritage site in 1982.

# CHAPTER TEN

# DIEGO GARCIA—"U.S. MALTA IN THE INDIAN OCEAN"

ALTHOUGH THE CONCEPT OF SEAPOWER has not entirely escaped change, its foundation, the sea, remains as significant as ever and varies little. The sea remains the most effective transportation highway on this planet. It covers almost three-quarters of the Earth's surface and, with few exceptions, is widely navigable.

At the time the British government had taken the decision to pull out east of Suez, secret negotiations were taking place between the Pentagon and Whitehall to acquire a strategic location for a U.S. Base, which would enable the United States to fill the vacuum the British would leave behind.

It was also becoming more and more apparent that the Soviet Union was taking more interest in the area. Until 1967, there were no Soviet naval vessels in the Indian Ocean, but by the end of 1968, a permanent presence had been established. Under the astute leadership of its former commander in Chief, Admiral Sergei G. Korshkov, the USSR's "seapower of the state" was transformed from little more than a coastal defence force into a first-magnitude blue water navy. Of course, Korshkov also understood the necessity for the Soviet Union to acquire access to overseas bases. He was crafting a navy to replicate an already demonstrated American capability for extension of seapower—thus national political influence—to salt water and land regions distant from the homeland.

In early 1965, Mauritius was beginning to make noises about

becoming independent. A Labour government was in office in London and its then Colonial Secretary Anthony Greenwood flew to the Mauritian capital with some startling news. The Mauritians, he said, could indeed have their independence from Britain, but only on condition that they gave up their claim to the islands of the Chagos archipelago, 1,200 miles away and in perpetuity. Mr. Greenwood gave no reason but offered three million Pounds in compensation which Prime Minister Sir Seewoosagur Ramgoolam and his cabinet eventually decided to accept. This accomplished, the colonial secretary then came to Seychelles and informed us that our three principal dependencies of Farquhar, Desroches, and Aldabra, would be detached and would in future constitute a brand-new colony to be named British Indian Ocean Territory (B.I.O.T.) and be administered by a commissioner who would be based at Victoria in Seychelles. In return, the British were to build for us an international airport on the island of Mahé so that we could develop our tourism.

It was more than a year before anyone realized why London had taken the time and trouble to set up a new dependent territory that was so scattered and so seemingly useless. On December 30, 1966, all was answered. Britain and the United States signed an exchange of notes, "…concerning the availability for defence purposes' of the islands. The notes were voluminous but essentially said one thing. The United States of America was given permission to lease the islands for fifty years (with an option of a further twenty) without payment and to build a defence installation there to suit such needs as might arise. Given the general instability of the region and the absolute necessity of guaranteeing the free flow of Gulf oil, Washington and London seized on the notion of keeping the islands of B.I.O.T. for their very own, in case the need arose.

I first learned that the Chagos islands had been chosen as the site for the American base in lieu of Aldabra from no other than Mr. Paul Moulinié, a Seychellois who served alongside me as a member of the Seychelles Executive Council, a body which could, more or less, be described as a cabinet in a British colonial administration. Mr. Moulinié was also the chief executive officer of the Chagos-Agalega Company, which operated from an office on Albert Street in Victoria opposite my family's supermarket. This tall and handsome man, who was always dressed in white, was certainly in an agitated mood when he came to see me in my own office, a five minutes' walk away. The reason was simple. Chagos-Agalega Company, a Seychelles registered company, which had a long-term lease with the government of Mauritius for the economic exploitation of the islands, had been approached and offered one million pounds for the Chagos archipelago. In return, they were to wind up the company and cease all operations on the island.

The decision of the British and the Americans to abandon Aldabra in favor of Diego Garcia was certainly a case where birds and tortoises won but men, women and children were made to suffer. No one has better written about the saga of the Chagos islanders than Simon Winchester in his book, *Outposts*[1]—*Journeys to the Surviving Relics of the British Empire:*

> On the day that British Indian Ocean Territory was formally established as a colony, the Chagos Islands were peopled by some 2,000 islanders—more than there were in the Falkland Islands at the same time, as many as there were on Tristan da Cunha, Ascension and Pitcairn put together, and half as many as on the island of Anguilla. They worked for a French-run copra and coconut oil company known as Chagos Agalega, and their little oil factories were fairly prosperous. "There were touches of old-fashioned ostentation" a visitor reported in the late 1950s. There was a château...whitewashed stores, factories, and workshops, shingled and thatched cottages clustered around the green...lamp standards and parked motor launches...
>
> And the inhabitants were all of them British subjects, citizens of a Crown colony, entitled to the protection and assistance of the Crown and, in the early days of their new status, governed on behalf of the Queen by the earl of Oxford and Asquith, the colony's first commissioner.

---

[1] *Outposts* by Simon Winchester was first published in the United Kingdom in 1985 by Hodder and Stoughton Ltd.

But they were to be given no protection or assistance, by the earl, the Crown, or anybody else. Instead the British government, obeying with craven servility the wishes of the Pentagon—by now the formal lessees of the island group—physically removed every man, woman, and child from the islands, and placed them, bewildered and frightened, on the islands of Mauritius and the Seychelles. The British officials did not consult the islanders. They did not tell them what was happening to them. They did not tell anyone else what they planned to do. They just went right ahead and uprooted an entire community, ordered people from their jobs and their homes, crammed them on to ships, and sailed them away to a new life in a new and foreign country. They trampled on two centuries of community and two centuries of history, and dumped the detritus into prison cells and on to quaysides in Victoria and Port Louis, and proceeded, with all the arrogant attitudes that seemed peculiar to this imperial rump, promptly to forget all about them.

Or would have done, had not David Ottaway, an enterprising reporter from the *Washington Post*, travelled to Mauritius in September 1975 and discovered, in a slum close to the Port Louis docks, an abject and indifferent group of more than a thousand islanders from the Chagos Archipelago. They called themselves the Ilois, and they told a horrifying story: They had been kidnapped en masse and turned out of their homes to make way for the American forces who, they understood, now had control of their islands.

The decision to build a U.S. base at Diego Garcia was not without opposition in the United States. In fact, Senator Kennedy fought the idea, charging it would ignite a "naval presence" in the Indian Ocean. The U.S. Congress was torn over the issue until it was disclosed that the Soviets were building a naval base at Berbera in Somalia. After these revelations and after a joint House-Senate Armed Services Committee delegation toured the area and returned with the report that a large number of Russian warships routinely navigated the Indian Ocean, Congress voted to provide funds for Diego Garcia. This base gave the United States important naval capability in the Indian Ocean. For one admiral, it was "the Malta of the Indian Ocean."

Simon Winchester, who arrived on the island of Diego Garcia

in the company of an Australian woman named Ruth Boydel, on a yacht, *Skatty Bell,* and was promptly issued with a "Go away order," was able to have a view of the Chagos lagoon with its gigantic assemblage of naval power and supplies.

This is how he described what he saw:

> I could count seventeen ships riding at anchor. Thirteen were cargo vessels stuffed to the gunwales with tanks and ammunition, fuel and water supplies, rockets and jeeps and armored personnel carriers, all ready to sail at two hours' notice. There was an atomic submarine, the USS *Corpus Christi*—a batch of crewmen were even now sailing by in their liberty boat off to see the delights of the rock and presumably to ferret out some of the eighty women assigned to the base; there was a submarine tender—USS *Proteus* which I had last seen in Holy Loch in Scotland, and which was packed with every last item, from a nut to a nuclear warhead, that a cruising submariner could ever need; and there was the strange white-painted former assault ship, the USS *La Salle,* now converted into a floating headquarters for the U.S. central command, and in the bowels of which admirals and generals played "games of survivable war in the Mid-East theater", with the white paint keeping their electronic battle directors and intelligence decoders cool in the Indian Ocean sun.

Diego Garcia is one of fifty-two islands in the Chagos Archipelago, which extends over an area of 10,000 square miles. The archipelago is located in the heart of the Indian Ocean, south of India and between Africa and Indonesia.

The tropical island is a narrow coral atoll with a land area of about eleven square miles, nearly enclosing a lagoon. Its configuration is that of a "V," drawn by a shaky hand. The island stretches thirty-seven miles from tip to tip, with an opening to the north-northwest. Three small islands dot the mouth of the lagoon, which is approximately thirteen miles long and up to six miles wide. The lagoon is from sixty to one hundred feet deep with numerous coral heads in most areas. Shallow reefs surround the island on the ocean side, as well as in the lagoon. The island's mean height above sea level is four feet.

The climate is typically tropical, with warm temperatures and high humidity throughout the year. The average yearly precipitation is 102 inches. Island flora is lush, consisting in large measure of coconut trees which were the staple of the island for 200 years. Additionally, there are a variety of other tropical plants and trees, including large hardwood trees such as takamaka, porcie, guyoid, and casa. I understand that care was taken during construction of the base to preserve the ecology of Diego Garcia as much as possible. Wildlife on the island is sparse, but interesting and varied. No dangerous wildlife exists on the islands. The worst of the lot is a small scorpion with a sting comparable to that of a bee. Land crabs, coconut crabs, and hermit crabs abound and you may see a coconut rat scurry about. The largest creatures are the approximately 300 donkeys whose ancestors worked the now-abandoned plantation in the days before mechanization.

\* \* \* \*

Thinking about the geo-politics of the Indian Ocean, one must not overlook the great design of the Americans and the British in involving Iran in getting this ocean to remain, as much as possible, a pro-Western lake. At that time the United States enjoyed close and friendly relations with His Imperial Majesty Shah Mohammed Reza Pahlavi and had succeeded to convince him that Iran could easily become one of the world's great naval powers, which would replace the British in patrolling, alongside the Americans, the maritime routes East of Suez. For this reason, the Shah purchased several second-hand U.S. Naval vessels thus using a significant part of his oil wealth in the pursuit of national grandeur and power on the international stage at the expense of much needed social and welfare development within the country.

On March 23, 1976, only a few months before the Seychelles was to become an independent Republic, the Shah on the occasion of the 50th Anniversary of his nation under the Pahlavi Dynasty, issued a statement, "A Saga Bright as Iran's Sky."

My warm salutations to the great Iranian nation; to the nation whose inexhaustible power has once again come to the fore in this magnificent ceremony marking the solidarity between the Shah and the Nation.

My salutations to the great monarchs and courageous commanders of Iran's history; to all Iranian women and men who have handed down the flag of our ancient monarchy from one generation to the next as if in fulfillment of a sacred trust.

My salutations to Reza Shah the Great, the renowned commander of Iran's history and founder of the Pahlavi Dynasty, the man who arose from among Iranians and thought of nothing but Iran. For Iran he lived and for Iran he died.

On the 50th Anniversary under Pahlavi rule, before the mausoleum of a great Iranian whose soul is with us, in the name of the standard-bearer of the Iranian monarchy, I renew the eternal covenant of the Pahlavi Dynasty with my Nation which I am honoured to lead:

Taking Iran's history as witness, I declare that we, the Pahlavi Dynasty, nurse no love but that for Iran, and no zeal but that for the dignity of Iranians; recognise no duty but that of serving our State and Nation…As the commander of this monarchy, I make a covenant with Iran's history that this golden epic of modern Iran will be carried on to complete victory, and that no power on earth shall ever be able to stand against the bond of steel between the Shah and the nation. We shall never again be caught unaware. The Nation and the Imperial Armed Forces, which come from the ranks of the people and derive their power from our inexhaustible national resources, are alert day in and day out to protect their country. No foreigner or his agents will ever have a chance to penetrate the unshakable structure of our national sovereignty because Iran's destiny is now shaped by Iranians and for Iranians – and this shall always be the case.

Iran today is an Iran of construction, an Iran of Faith, confidence and hope, an Iran of humanism and s piritual maturity. This is a role, which we play not only domestically but also on a global scale. We know well and so do all other nations of the world that Iran today is a powerful State whose economic, political and military might is increasing daily and which enjoys unprecedented international prestige…"

A few weeks after these celebrations, I found myself on an official visit to Iran, which had been orchestrated, for me by the British and the Americans. In Teheran I paid a short courtesy call on His Majesty at the Imperial Palace before having a series of meetings with Ministers of the Iranian Cabinet under the Prime Ministership of the able and brilliant, Amir Abbas Hovedas. This visit culminated in the signing of an agreement for close economic and political collaboration between the Kingdom of Iran and the Republic of Seychelles as soon as Seychelles would become an independent nation.

Not surprising the Iranian Naval flotilla was the most impressive naval contingent in Port Victoria during our Independence celebrations. Unfortunately in less than a year a coup d'etat deposed me as President of Seychelles whilst attending another great Royal fiesta this time in London, the Jubilee of Her Majesty Queen Elizabeth II. At that time, I had hoped, considering the document I had signed in Teheran, that the Shah of Iran would assist me to restore constitutional Government in Seychelles. However, only a few days after the Coup, the Shah issued a statement that his Government saw no reason to interfere with the situation in Seychelles, "so long as Iranian's national interest is not threatened." It is ironical but true that only a year later, the Shah himself was overthrown and that President Carter lost no time to declare that the United States would not interfere with the changed situation in Iran "so long as U.S. national interest is not threatened."

The Shah assumed absolute power in Iran in 1953 when with the assistance of the U.S. Central Intelligence Agency, Prime Minister Mohammed Mossadeg was deposed. The Shah used his oil wealth to modernise the Nation which allowed women to vote and hold jobs—and created a more secular society. However, many Iranians who were devout Muslims were unhappy with these changes and many close to the Shah were corrupt. Anyone who disagreed with the Shah was forced to leave the Nation or faced savak, the Shah's brutal Police Force. A popular revolution in 1979 forced the Shah to flee the country and resulted in the return of Ayatollah Ruhollah Khomeini, an Islamic cleric, who had been in exiled in France. The Ayatollah, who gained control over the Nation, turned it into an Islamic Republic. Soon after he was denouncing the United States as "The Great Satan." When the United States allowed the Shah to come to New York City for cancer treatment, Iranians students stormed the American Embassy in Teheran and held 52 Americans for more than a year. Iran released the hostages in 1981 but tensions have continued to exist between the two Nations.

The average American today may not know it, but the Iranian Embassy in Washington, D.C. during the last years of the Shah's rule was the preferred home of Washington high society with the flamboyant Ambassador Ardeshir Zahedi regularly holding feasts, playing "Caviar Diplomacy."

I was, a few years ago, a guest of this former Representative of the Shah at a dinner he hosted at his "Villa de Roses" in Montreux, Switzerland, where he has been residing since the Shah was overthrown, and in our discussions, we could not help finding common grounds for questioning many aspects of U.S. Foreign Policy particularly with respect to the situation in the Middle East.

\* \* \* \*

Following the overthrow of the Shah of Iran in 1979, Diego Garcia saw the most dramatic build-up of any location since the Vietnam war era. In the spring of 1980, a large monetary appropriations bill was passed by the U.S. Congress to expand island facilities to meet future operational requirements.

In 1986, Diego Garcia became fully operational with the completion of a five hundred million construction program. According to the U.S. navy support facility information,[2] the 1990 Iraqi invasion of Kuwait marked the most intense operational period in Diego Garcia's history. From August 1, 1990 to February 28, 1991, NAVSUPPFAC Diego Garcia achieved and maintained the highest degree of operational readiness and provided levels of

---

[2] www.militarycity.com

support which outstripped all contingency planning. As the base population doubled almost overnight with the deployment of a strategic air command bombardment wing and other aviation detachments, workload base wide, increased from 300 to 2000 percent over peacetime levels with no personnel augmentation, and Diego Garcia became the only U.S. navy base that launched offensive air operations during Operation Desert Storm.

At the non-aligned summit meeting held in Durban from August 29 to September 3, 1998, the prime minister of Mauritius, Mr. Navin Ramgoolam, called for the restoration of Mauritius sovereignty over the Chagos Archipelago. He stated that the assumption of sovereignty by Britain over the islands in 1965 was illegal because it was contrary to Resolution 1514 of the General Assembly of the United Nations, which forbids the dismembering of a state before it achieves independence.

No doubt, Diego Garcia will remain the vital link in the U.S. Defence structure in the years ahead. Following the Falklands War, Rear Admiral J. Hanks, who commanded U.S. Middle East forces during the time that I was president of Seychelles, wrote that if it was not for the island of Ascension in the Atlantic, it would have been almost impossible for Britain to recover the Falklands. Hanks deduced that small islands can serve as unsinkable aircraft carriers with both offensive and defensive capabilities. This rationale helps to explain the strategic importance of the Seychelles islands with its 110 small islands including Aldabra scattered among more than two hundred thousand square miles of ocean.

# CHAPTER ELEVEN

# ON THE ROAD TO INDEPENDENCE

PARTY POLITICS IN SEYCHELLES developed against a background of Britain's decision to dismantle its empire; to pull out east of Suez and to allow the United States to fill up the vacuum she was leaving behind by first building a tracking station on Mahé and then establishing a vital base in Diego Garcia. Think of the concept of "strategic territory"; remind yourself of the atmosphere of the Cold War with the CIA and KGB at loggerheads, and you get more or less a clear picture of the scenario. Add to this, the introduction of "one man, one vote" democracy and all the political demagoguery which goes with it, and you have a little nation divided against itself; confused about the way ahead; not exactly certain under which sphere of influence it will be best to fall.

The Democratic Party under my leadership took the view that the devil we knew was better than the one we did not know and professed the policy of staying put with the United Kingdom. Aiming for the sky in order to get above the trees, I called for full integration with the United Kingdom. That was prompted by my conviction that Seychellois nationalism should be pursued on the basis of what was in the best interest of the average Seychellois, rather than in the interest of a few who were seeking the position of power. I did not believe the average Seychellois understood the issue before them and the important choice they were going to make about their future.

I thought it was funny for those advocating independence to

proclaim themselves "freedom fighters" when the United Kingdom had already publicly declared her commitments to: "…give effect to the wish of the colonial people."

Despite the excitement and the pride of having one's own flag, national anthem and currency which independence would bring, I questioned the wisdom of 75,000 people achieving meaningful nationhood in an age of international tension, mafiosi penetration, terrorism menace, and monetary instability. I could also see the potential of a foreign exchange problem, the problem of higher education, and the potential for a coup d'etat.

It so came to pass that the Democratic Party, with its policy of Integration, won two elections fought on the basis of universal adult suffrage, and that I served as chief minister of the islands from 1970 to 1975 when I became prime minister. Just after the last election, the British decided to replace their governor, Sir Bruce Greatbatch (who had been appointed governor and commander in chief of Seychelles following a distinguished career as secretary to the premier of northern Nigeria in 1959 and as deputy high commissioner in Kenya in 1964) to replace him by the relatively unknown Mr. Colin Allen, a New Zealander who had spent most of his career in different colonies of the Pacific. I thought there was in this appointment a message that we should think of taking our destiny in our own hands.

To think about it, previous Governors had included Sir Selwyn-Clarke who was director of medical services in Hong Kong during World War II and became the principal medical officer in the Ministry of Health in London following his time in Seychelles; Sir Frederick Crawford who became deputy governor of Kenya before becoming the governor of Uganda and subsequently became chairman of Anglo-American Corporation in Southern Africa; Lord Oxford and Asquith, the grandson of a former British prime minister, and Sir Hugh Norman Walker who left Seychelles to become governor of Hong Kong and now suddenly we were to receive a gentleman who was practically unknown in Westminster.

On the occasion of the swearing-in ceremony of Mr. Allen as governor and commander in chief, in my capacity as prime minister, I called upon him to request Her Majesty's government to stop playing with our future and to take steps to give effect to the desire of the majority of our people for closer links with the United Kingdom.

Governor Allen in his return address made no comment on this point. However, the next day, he invited me to come and meet with him at Government House. He told me that the Foreign Office was desirous to have a confidential meeting with me and that I should make arrangements to go to London in a private capacity as soon as possible.

A week later, I was at the Churchill Hotel, Portman Square in London. I had hardly unpacked my bags when Mr. Dennis Greenam knocked on my door and introduced himself. He was a man of medium height. He had a slight limp and a pleasant smile, by no means the stuffy colonial office type.

I gave him a drink and waited curiously to hear what he had to say. After explaining who he was—an adviser on decolonization to Her Majesty's government, he had been closely involved in the development towards independence of Kenya, Zambia, and Mauritius—he wasted no time in coming to the point.

"I've been following the situation in Seychelles," he said. I must tell you that in light of your speech when you welcomed the Governor..." I looked hard at him. Were we to get our answer at last?

"All these years you have been talking about integration. I must make it clear that this is a proposition which the British government is unwilling to consider."

Briefly, I closed my eyes. So, after all these years, I had finally got an answer. And it was the wrong one. There was no doubt in my mind that Greenam was indeed speaking on behalf of the British Government and I listened in silence as he continued. First of all, he tried to soften the blow.

Her Majesty's government profoundly admired my pro-British stance and felt that, as a gesture of courtesy, I should be quietly informed of its decision. If the policy had been announced publicly, it would embarrass me and allow my opponents to make political capital. An official announcement would appear to be a rebuff.

Then he outlined what he saw as the political realities. Tapping out the points on his fingers he spelled them out. "Look, Mr. Mancham, you have a majority on the islands at the moment but your opponents are receiving massive financial aid from outside, and one day they may well be voted into office, and since integration is not on, I suggest you go for a policy of independence as early as possible."

For a few moments I could say nothing; then I tried another tactic. What about associated statehood, I asked? I knew that arrangement had been made with certain Caribbean islands, which had become self-governing while Britain had retained sovereignty and the responsibility for foreign affairs, law and order and defence.

Greenam slowly shook his head. "Not after Anguilla", he said. I remembered the story. Britain had granted self-government to the Caribbean islands of St. Kitts-Nevis and Anguilla in 1967. In June of that year, Anguilla unilaterally declared its independence. There was trouble on the island and the British were forced to send a warship.

He shook my hand and left me feeling saddened. I had known deep down for some time that integration was unlikely but had thought that the United Kingdom, with all her vast diplomatic experience, would have worked out some formula which would keep us closely linked to her. After all, France had declared Reunion as one of its départements, and far out in the Pacific, Hawaii had become a state of the United States. It was only a question of will. But no. There was no choice left for poor Seychelles. Independence was inevitable and we would just have to face it with calmness and dignity.

A few minutes after Greenam had left, the phone rang.

"Mr. Mancham? Fox Tolbert here." The accent was clipped, a military voice.

"Who?"

"I think you are expecting me, sir."

I couldn't place the name. "What did you say your name was?"

"Fox Tolbert, sir. In the lobby. I'd like to come up and have a word with you. Between ourselves. May I come up?"

I agreed. A few minutes later, he walked in, looking for all the world like something out of a James Bond film. He was tall and well-built, smartly dressed and wearing a club tie, very much an ex-service officer.

"May I have a look around first?" he asked as we shook hands.

"Carry on," I said.

He looked under the table and chairs, checked the television, then disappeared into the bathroom. He looked satisfied.

"In this electronic age," he said by way of explanation, "you never know what might be around." When he was settled, he began to explain. "I belong to a group of prominent businessmen who are strongly opposed to the spread of Communism."

I looked at him, thinking maybe I was in the middle of a bad movie.

"We have been studying developments in Seychelles," he continued, "and we are fully satisfied that Albert René is in the pay of the Communists. In view of this, my committee has decided to provide your party with a monthly allowance. Can't say how much this will be yet, but if you can give me your London bank account number, I'll see that the money is promptly and regularly deposited."

"These businessmen of yours," I said. "Do I know any of them personally?"

He shook his head. "Sir, I'm sorry to say that my committee must remain totally unknown. Indeed, if you were to take any initiative to find out who we are, then that would be the end of our association. Nor must you tell any of your supporters about this meeting."

With that he wrote down an address and box number in Oxford and left. I sat down and tried to work it all out. I remembered a few weeks earlier meeting a man called Major Geoffrey Dawson. He had been introduced to me by Dougy Mott, our security adviser, who was an Englishman. Later on Mott had whispered to me that Dawson was from MI6 and was known within the organization as the "Galloping Ghost."

Could there be a connection between Mott, Dawson, and Fox Tolbert? Could this strange man who had just left me be from M16? It had obviously been a bad news-good news scenario. First Greenam had supplied the shock, then Fox Tolbert had provided the first-aid cream. You have no choice but to go for independence, they were saying, but don't worry, you are not alone Their plan had worked. Before they arrived, I was still hopeful about integration, but now, only an hour later, I was resigned to independence and relieved that some people were taking an interest in us. There and then I decided to do as Fox Tolbert said; I never did try to find out who the businessmen were and soon the first anonymous contribution turned up in my account.

Now there was no need to stay longer in London. I cut my visit short, caught the next flight back home and called a meeting of the party's national executives to tell them Greenam's message.

They were united in thinking that, if Britain was determined to lead us into independence, then we must try to form the first independent government, despite all those years of fighting against it. We had no choice and there was no point beating our heads against a brick wall.

That night, I went to Radio Seychelles to explain the situation to the people. I was tempted to talk about Britain's hypocrisy but I said nothing. Fox Tolbert's visit had convinced me that Britain wanted us to win any forthcoming election and I decided that this was not the time to attack her.

At that time, I never truly knew what Washington, D.C. was thinking about these developments. Recently, Raymond Seitz[1] (who started his political career at the U.S. Embassy in Nairobi as a

---

[1]Raymond Seitz was born in Honolulu, Hawaii. After graduating from Yale, he joined the U.S. Foreign Service in 1966. He held posts in Canada and Africa. and was three times assigned to the American embassy in London, on the last occasion as ambassador. He resigned from the post in 1994. In 2002, Mr. Seitz is vice chairman of Lehman Brothers International in Europe and he serves on several corporate boards in Britain and the United States. He and his wife, Caroline, live in London.

junior political officer with responsibility for the Seychelles and ended it as the first career diplomat ever appointed American ambassador to the court of St. James) published his book, *Over Here,*[2] in which he made the following observation about the politics of Seychelles:

> Everywhere else in the world, populations had been agitating for independence from their colonial masters and sometimes starting wars to achieve it, but in Seychelles, the politics were upside down. The colonial masters wanted to impose independence on the islands and the local politicians were doing everything they could to resist it. The Seychelles were one of the leftovers in Britain's withdrawal from east of Suez, but London had a problem shooing the Seychellois puppy from the imperial lap. The British no longer wanted responsibility for the islands because they had spent too much money there, which is exactly why the islanders wanted to remain colonized. These politics did not make much difference to the United States, so long as the tracking station on top of the mountain could continue to emit and receive signals from outer space.

Sadly, Seitz made no mention about how I got involved with the CIA.

The people of Seychelles took my broadcast about the change of policy to independence quietly. Our supporters were naturally profoundly disappointed. Overnight, their dream of remaining secure under the British umbrella was shattered and a question mark about our security had appeared on the horizon.

The next day, Governor Allen announced that an election would be held in April 1974 and thus began our election campaign. Now that the question of independence was no longer an issue, the main argument centered on which party was the more honest, more capable and more fit to govern, which meant that the campaign was a jamboree of character assassination. The Democratic Party support, as always, came from the better-educated part of the community and the women. While the SPUP was strongest

---

[2] Which was published by Widenfeld and Nicholson (1998).

among the poorer section where their seductive rich-versus-poor approach had maximum impact.

If you have not been in politics, it is difficult to explain the psychological campaign. There is some kind of irrational energy, some natural amphetamine rush to finish. There is often a passion about running for office, a focus as narrow and intense as ambition, a desire as great as a love affair. Such exciting opportunities naturally disappear from the moment democracy is killed and the one-party state dictatorship takes over.

On election day, April 24, there was an air of strange calm in contrast with the turbulent days of campaigning. Democracy was at work. It was as if a crucial trial had taken place and the nation was waiting the verdict of the jury. When the results were announced, the Democratic Party had won thirteen of the fifteen National Assembly seats but when translated into popular votes, we had won by only 53 percent to 47 percent. It was that close, but by all democratic precedence, it was a clear majority.

# CHAPTER TWELVE

# OF GEO-POLITICS AND THE CIA'S INVOLVEMENT

FOLLOWING THE ELECTION, the British government hosted a constitutional conference in London to decide on a new constitution which would eventually lead the country to full independence. At the urging of the Labour government in London, I agreed that now that the independence issue was over, we should all work in the interest of the peaceful development of the islands. I, therefore, accepted the suggestion of forming a coalition government with the SPUP—with myself becoming the prime minister and Mr. René and some other SPUP personalities becoming substantive ministers in our cabinet. During that period of the coalition leading to independence, the SPUP played as good as gold and collaborated fully in the day to day running of the country. About a year later, we attended another Constitutional Conference in London. At that time, four main decisions were taken. The first was that Britain would return to us the three islands which included Aldabra and which together with the Chagos Archipelago had been made to constitute the British Indian Ocean Territory. The second decision was that the country on independence day would become a republic. Thirdly, that James Richard Marie Mancham would be in the constitution named as the first president of the republic and enjoy that position up to when the next election was due. Fourthly, that the Seychelles would become an independent and sovereign nation on June 29, 1976.

The closer we came to independence, the more aware we became of the strategic importance of our islands. This was clearly demonstrated by the sudden interest the superpowers were taking in us. Besides Britain and France, China, India, the USSR and, indeed, the United States announced that they wanted to open up diplomatic relationship and each one set up an embassy—all these embassies on our coconut islands with a population of less than 75,000 people.

One morning in my office, I found myself facing a middle-aged American who had arrived. To my secretary, he was the first secretary at the U.S. embassy in Nairobi but he lost no time in telling me who he really was—an employee of the CIA.

"In the long term," said the American, who shall be known as Mr. X, "we have our plans for the Indian Ocean. Iran will be used to fill the gap caused by British withdrawal. We also wish to secure your independence as fast as possible."

I listened, fascinated, as he continued. "You have the tracking station on Mahé. We are busy building our base on Diego Garcia next door. We want to keep it this way but the Soviets and their proxies will plot for your overthrow."

Mr. X wanted me to sign a document authorizing the CIA to organize our intelligence system, which would allow them to keep an eye on local groups, which, in his opinion, were out to make trouble for us, the region, and, therefore, for the United States. In addition, he wanted to support the ultimate build-up of a para-military unit. "The sums involved for such an operation would be substantial and would have to come from Washington, but within the Nairobi budget, I can only arrange to train a small nucleus of bodyguards for you."

It was Monday, June 28, 1976 and midnight was almost upon us. The Royal party had long since taken their seats in the new stadium. There had been stirring performances from the Royal marine band and the band of the Indian navy. Local school children had given a display of club twirling, police dogs had gone through their paces, the Roman Catholic and Anglican bishops had each offered a short prayer, René and I had made our speeches;

and now, precisely thirty seconds to midnight, in total darkness, the flag party made up of members of the Seychelles police force made its way to the center of the stadium. The place was packed but there was not a whisper. Precisely on time, at one minute to midnight, a spotlight was snapped on illuminating the flagpole in a single beam picking up the Union Jack. Simultaneously, the Marine band started up with *God Save the Queen*. I stood beneath the pole next to Governor Allen with René on his left watching as the Union Jack was slowly hauled down. As the Union Jack disappeared out of the spotlight, the new Seychelles flag appeared in its place, red and blue with a white diagonal cross and our new crest—a giant tortoise and a coconut palm in the centre—rising slowly up the pole. Once it was secured, the band struck up our new national anthem. Beyond, I could see the harbor glittering with floodlit warships from five countries: the United States, France, Iran, India, and Australia.

It was zero hour. Our little group of islands had been born a nation. My feelings were mixed. In that half second, I had left behind the role of prime minister in a colony and became president of an independent republic. Suddenly, Seychelles was alone in a world of conflict and pressure.

It was a well-known fact, though, that my newly declared policy of "friend to all and enemy to none" was more the result of pressure and circumstances. Although, I was officially non-aligned, deep down I remained very much pro-West. This sentiment was openly manifested when on July 4, 1976, only a few days after our independence, we issued a set of stamps, despite several milestone in the U.S. history, to commemorate the bicentennial depicting the 200th anniversary of America's independence. As a local newspaper stated, "They are among the first Seychelles stamps to bear the effigy of President Mancham and they go a long way to testify to the prevailing friendship and understanding between the Republic of Seychelles and the United States of America."

From all appearances, the coalition government had fostered an image of a stable paradise and our airport was becoming busier and busier with our hotel beds at a premium. A fantastic investment climate prevailed; there was no unemployment; the standard of living shot up; new houses sprouted out of the ground like spring flowers; more cars appeared on the roads and traffic jams were a new problem. Most of all, the Seychellois were becoming proud. The happiness of the people was a prime objective of our policy.

Some months after our independence, I was on an official visit in Paris when I received a message that Prince Talal of Saudi Arabia was in Vienna and urgently wanted to see me. The next morning I was boarding a private plane at Le Bourget sent for me by the prince. As I fastened my seat belt, I wondered why he was taking the trouble to fly me to Austria. I had met the man only once, a few weeks earlier, when he had visited Seychelles together with Adnan Khashoggi. He was interested in buying the bay of Port Launay where he wanted to build hotels and a marina—to develop the place into a complex which, in his words, "…would rival Marbella."

I remembered him as being a quiet and shrewd man. I learned that he was the brother of King Khalid and a favorite son of Abdul Aziz, the founder of modern day Saudi Arabia. He was most definitely a man to be taken seriously.

Soon I found myself at the Imperial Hotel opposite him in flowing robes. He told me that he had to come to Austria for a medical checkup. I nodded and waited for him to come to the point. "Mr. President," he said, "I want to thank you for the welcome you gave me in Seychelles. It is a beautiful country and I like your people. I want to invest a lot of money but there is a problem …I don't like the look in the eyes of your prime minister …"

As soon as I got back to Paris, I looked up Mr. X's number. In the few months since his promise of help for our internal security, I had regularly been in touch, asking him to tell me when something concrete would happen. The first time I called him, he was apologetic. "Look, Mr. Mancham," he said, "President Ford has got Senator Church looking into the CIA. We are being torn apart at the moment. With the disgrace of Watergate and the guilt over Vietnam, the country wants to have a go at us."

He became quite poetic as he continued, "The country is flaying itself with moral whips. It's become fashionable to purge every part of the system."

"Where does this leave us?" I asked.

"At the moment, in limbo," he said. "We've been told here in Nairobi to delay the project for three months until things calm down."

That had been the first phone call. But it was not the last. I had called him again in the autumn. This time, the problem was the presidential election.

"I'm sorry, Mr. Mancham, but the climate isn't right. During a presidential election, Washington doesn't give high priority to foreign policy matters."

Jimmy Carter's victory in November 1976 led to yet another call.

"As you know," said Mr. X, "during the election campaign, the role of the CIA became a controversial issue. We now have to wait for President-Elect Carter to evolve his philosophy towards us."

I think I swore down the line.

"We guarantee, however, that in two or three months' time, things will start moving."

Two months later, things did start moving—but in the wrong direction. In January, Carter's nominee for the directorship of the CIA, Theodore Sorensen, asked the president to withdraw his nomination. Sorensen had run into opposition from some senators who objected to him on the grounds that, as a confidante of the Kennedys, he had taken classified material—when on the White House staff in 1964—and used it in a book he had written on the Kennedy administration.

A few days later, Admiral Stanville Turner, a former classmate of Jimmy Carter was nominated as CIA director. So, Mr. X who had telephoned me to inform me of this decision assured me that now things would start moving.

# CHAPTER THIRTEEN

# SURVIVAL IN EXILE

THREE FORTY-FIVE IN THE MORNING is a bad time for telephones to ring, unless the caller is a beautiful woman or a close friend—preferably both. Telephones should be silent after eight in the evening. In the middle of the night, it is usually trouble.

I was in a deep sleep, a heavy contented slumber in a suite of the Savoy Hotel, the guest of Her Majesty's government, invited in my capacity as president of the new Republic of Seychelles to take part in the Queen's twenty-fifth jubilee celebrations. It was June 5, 1977. In two days' time, I was due to address the Commonwealth Heads of Government Conference, honored to be chosen to answer Prime Minister James Callaghan's speech of welcome.

I reached for the phone, idly wondering who was calling, aware that hotel operators, especially such guardians of privacy as those of the Savoy, are reluctant to disturb their guests.

"President Mancham?"

The tone of voice was apologetic.

"Mr. Adnan Khashoggi has been trying to get in touch with you. Could you please call him urgently at his Paris number?"

Khashoggi? What on earth did he want? I had met him some years before and we had become good friends. I knew him as an astonishing character, one of the world's richest businessmen and supposedly the model for and inspiration of Harold Robin's book, *The Pirate*.

I was wide awake by the time the call came through and I snatched at the receiver. Adnan came straight to the point. He was sorry to wake me but there had been a coup in my country. Slowly and precisely, he told me that he had been talking to the captain of his yacht, the *Khalidia*, which was moored in Port Victoria, Seychelles. The man had heard on his radio that shots had been fired and a curfew imposed, that the Seychelles constitution had been raped and that I had been deposed as president of the Republic of Seychelles. I immediately thought about some help and assistance to restore constitutionality and, of course, among others, I thought of Mr. X.

Meanwhile in Seychelles, a large contingent of Tanzanian soldiers had flown in to consolidate the Socialist takeover and the man who was only the day before my prime minister was now the de facto President. René criticized my "flamboyant lifestyle" and said that I had spent too much time jet-setting and not enough minding the affairs of state.

I will answer these accusations by quoting from David Lamb's best seller, *The Africans:*[1]

> But if Mancham pursued the good life with gusto, he also worked tirelessly on behalf of the Seychelles. He was a one-man public-relations agency, travelling the world and telling anyone who would listen about the beauty of a nation very few people had ever heard of. He opened an international airport and several luxury hotels sprang up. The tourist industry boomed, visitors arrived from distant corners of the world to enjoy this tropical paradise whose president had a special credo he called, "The Singing Philosophy"—just be happy as a person and a nation. His goal, Mancham declared, was to put a boy with a guitar under every palm tree...
>
> Without Mancham, the Seychelles might have remained an isolated backwater. But his great failing was naïveté, his belief that his country was entitled to something that did not belong to Africa—an age of innocence.

---

[1] *The Africans* was part political travelogue and part contemporary history. The book was the result of four years spent in Africa by the *Los Angeles Times* correspondent, David Lamb. First published in hardcover by Ramdom House in 1982. The part dealing with Seychelles and myself was specially selected by *Readers' Digest* and published in twenty languages.

With France and Britain having recognized the new government in Seychelles and with the CIA having told me that they would find me if and when they needed me, my first preoccupation was how to survive in exile with honor and dignity. I had invested some money outside Seychelles but I knew that from then on, I would be living in a situation of depleting assets, unless I was to find some gainful occupation. I dreaded the idea of a drastic drop in the quality of life which I had known. As chief minister, prime minister and president of the islands, I had made many friends. Those among them I thought would run away, did so faster than expected. Among those I thought would stay, some still did run away and that hurt. Fortunately, those who remained were really true friends!

Lars-Eric Lindblad, the ebullient Swedish-American voyager, showman and scholar whom I had befriended in the sixties when his cruise-ship, the *Lindblad Explorer,* arrived in Port Victoria was one of those friends who took the initiative to call me soon after he had heard about the coup: "Jimmy," he said, "There will always be a cabin for you on any cruise of the *Lindblad Explorer.* The only thing I ask in return is that you preserve your high spirits and joie de vivre and make our passengers happy."

Throughout my life in exile, I am sure many people must have gazed at the optimistic look on my entrepreneurial face and concluded that I had made a few million dollars. These people, may of course, have never realized that I have always lived with the spirit of that fisherman who wakes up every morning full of optimism that today is the day when he will catch the prized fish. At the end of the trip, if he has caught sufficient sardines, and enough mackerels to pay for his expenses and feed his family, there is nothing to stop him going to bed and dreaming that tomorrow will be the day when he will, in fact, bring home that prized catch.

Of course, this is the operational base of the modern entrepreneur. In this world of free enterprise, big money is being made by people every day. The importance is to enjoy the pursuit with the spirit of that fisherman. If a big deal is made, nobody is going to be sad about it but while the big deal remains outstanding, be happy with the small ones, which bring in the bread and butter, pay for the petrol, and, together with the facilities of the credit card, enable you to take the family on the annual holiday.

It was against this philosophical premise that I faced every day of my life in exile. I had also learned that we live today in a world where things do not just happen but are made to happen by men of goodwill and vision who see an opportunity and then decide to collaborate to turn dreams into reality. At the end of the day, when an edifice has been created, it is wonderful to be able to look at it and to know we have shared in its creation and, perhaps more importantly, that we have made some money to keep going if not to grow.

Backed with such an attitude, I became active internationally—promoting joint ventures and the transfer of technology, the organization of project financing, and, along the way, benefited from a few trading opportunities. Among my successes was the promotion of a joint venture for the exploitation of a marginal oil field in offshore Canada between a company in Halifax, Nova Scotia and a North Sea company in United Kingdom I became President of a small but lucrative airline in Germany, in which capacity I benefited from cheap travel and a generous expense account. I also got involved in the selling of islands worldwide[2]—one of them which brought me a good commission was Galloo Island, in Jefferson County, New York. It was one of the largest private islands in the United States, located in eastern Lake Ontario, twelve miles offshore from Sackett's Harbor Yacht Club, and only six miles from the Canadian border. I was also associated with the sale of Robins Island (about which I researched and wrote a booklet), situated fifty-six miles east of Kennedy Airport in the Hamptons, off Long Island, in the State of New York. After the opening up of China, I accompanied several German business groups to Beijing, Shanghai and Hangzhou negotiating and promoting joint ven-

[2] I was closely associated with René Boehm and Farhad Vladi who had founded the agency for private islands: 'Boehm and Vladi'. With their encouragement and support, I produced a coffee table book entitled *Island Splendor* which carried a forward by Prince Bernhard of the Netherlands in 1980.

tures of all kinds. China was not an easy place to do business. There were some successes and some failures but I always took the experience as a part of the learning process.

God willing, I hope to find the time to write a book about my experience among different entrepreneurs.

My agenda was always full. If I was not on business travel, then I would be on lecture tours. The first lecture I delivered was on October 31, 1983 at the Union Society of Cambridge University in the United Kingdom. I spoke on the theme, "Struggle for Power in the Indian Ocean." Afterwards, I had a contract with Keedick Lecture Bureau of New York City run by Robert Keedick who organized for me several lecture circuits to different parts of the United States.

With so many opportunities before me, I had little time left for Seychelles politics. In fact, I was jumping from one plane to another as if to prove that if René had taken over the Seychelles, I was myself in the process of conquering the world. However, news coming from the islands were not good. René, after the coup, moved the islands to the left politically and declared it a one-party state. He partly nationalized the economy; compulsorily acquired properties without paying compensation; locked up opponents and caused many of them to flee in exile while he formed an army first with the help of Tanzanian soldiers, then with Malagasy and finally with soldiers from North Korea. The influx of tourists slowed, the economy weakened, the free press died, every year on the anniversary of his coup, this would be observed with a military parade through downtown Victoria—our little capital. There were uniformed soldiers, armored personnel and lots of weapons everywhere. As David Lamb so aptly put it in *The Africans,* "The palm trees along the mute swayed in the balmy breezes and under them, were young men who had forgotten their guitars and now carried guns."

In November 1981, a group of Seychellois in exile got involved with Mike Hoare, the notorious Irishman, who had fought in the Congo in the sixties. Fifty-two white mercenaries led by Hoare flew into Victoria on a commercial jetliner pretending to represent a sport and drinking club called, The Ancient Order of Foam Blowers. A custom officer discovered their weapons while checking baggage and after an exchange of fire at the airport, the mercenaries hijacked an Air India plane and flew back to South Africa—the coup attempt nipped in the bud. Although they said that their initiative was aimed at bringing me back to power, I must say I had nothing to do with it.

These developments, of course, made headline news and I was even summoned to the United Nations in New York to appear before a commission, which had been appointed to investigate the circumstances around the hijacking of the Air India plane. Throughout this time, western governments ignored the plight of the Seychellois people. It was obvious that as long as Mr. René did not interfere with the tracking station, it would be business as usual despite so many declarations and utterances from Washington about democracy and human rights.

# CHAPTER FOURTEEN

# THE GRENADA ADVENTURE AND THE END OF THE COLD WAR

IN OCTOBER 1983, I BECAME VERY ANGRY when President Reagan ordered American troops to invade the Caribbean island of Grenada. There, Prime Minister Maurice Bishop, had imitated exactly what President René was doing in Seychelles and like, Mr. René, he was cozying up to Cuba. Of course, President Reagan went to Grenada at a time when he needed to boost his popularity with the American people. I had no problem with this, but when he justified his intervention by saying that he could not allow Marxist penetration within "our hemisphere," I wrote to him questioning where his hemisphere started and where it ended. I pointed out that the Seychelles, with a sophisticated U.S. tracking station on top of its main island and a Diego Garcia nuclear naval base nearby had, in essence, become as much a part of the American hemisphere as Grenada.

The night after the American invasion of Grenada had become news, I watched a program on British television with Sir Shridath Ramphal, secretary general of the commonwealth going out of his way to severely criticise President Reagan's action in Grenada. I thought it was opportune for me to make a few points and wrote to *The Times* of London as follows:

> Sir Shridath Ramphal, secretary general of the commonwealth, last night on British TV criticized U.S. actions in Grenada. What a lot of hypocrisy. Seychelles was a full member of the com-

monwealth and I was attending the Commonwealth Heads of State Conference when my government was overthrown by a violent coup which had been planned and prepared in Tanzania—which country flew in several contingent of soldiers. The secretary general of the commonwealth did not say a word about the rape of the democratic constitution of the Seychelles and its military occupation by another member of his organization. Today, there are hundreds of North Korean soldiers assisting the Tanzanians and the Marxist René in oppressing the people of Seychelles. There have been cases of disappearances, mass arrest, imprisonment without trial, and hundreds have fled to live in exile. But up to now not a word from Sir Shridath Ramphal.

The British MPs who attacked President Reagans' actions are also guilty, of the same hypocrisy and double standard. I was in London also to attend the jubilee of Her Majesty who is head of the commonwealth. Seychelles had been a British colony for over 200 years and became independent following free elections under a constitutional instrument which had been passed by the British Parliament and assented to by Her Majesty, the Queen. Did anyone of the MPs say a word about the rape of this constitution and the military occupation by Tanzania? In fact, only one year after our tragedy, Prime Minister James Callaghan was welcoming and feasting René in London thereby compounding his treachery and condoning his treason.

Where lies the difference between North Korean soldiers in Seychelles and U.S. marines in Grenada? At least everybody knows that Grenada is on the U.S. doorstep but North Korea is two continents and five oceans away from Seychelles. Perhaps Sir Shridath Ramphal can answer this question and explain his silence over Seychelles."

On January 16, 1984, President Ronald Reagan delivered a speech which was broadcast live throughout Western Europe—which for the first time, sounded conciliatory towards the Soviet Union. He said that if the Soviet government behaved itself domestically by starting to reform its oppressive system and to operate with civility in international affairs, he would lower the tension level. He insisted that his goal was compromise and not confrontation and that the American and Soviet people had far more in common than the political and economic systems which divided their governments.

On March 11, 1985, Mikhail Gorbachev, who had welcomed Reagan's new tone was chosen general secretary of the Soviet Communist Party and leader of the Soviet Union. Reagan and Gorbachev held their first summit meeting on November 19th to 21, 1985 in Geneva. When the two men met again, on October 11 and 12, 1986 in Reykjavik, Iceland it was obvious that we were approaching the end of the Cold War. I thought the time had come to call for the restoration of democracy in Seychelles.

On December 9, 1987, President Reagan received President Gorbachev at the White House and signed the agreement for the scrapping of intermediate-range nuclear missiles. Although President Reagan had not replied to my letter concerning Grenada when I had questioned as to where his hemisphere started and where it ended, I thought it would be a good thing to send President Reagan a letter of congratulations:

Dear President Reagan,

Warmest congratulations to you and the Soviet leader Mikhail Gorbachev on the historic signing of the Agreement scrapping intermediate-range nuclear missiles. Any step towards world peace and order and the lessening of big power rivalry must be welcomed by people of goodwill the world over—not in the least the people of some small islands in the Indian Ocean (The Seychelles) who have over the last *twenty years* been the direct victims of such rivalry.

In your TV address to the Soviet people last night, you, Mr. President of the United States, chose to emphasize the importance that you, your government and people attach to the principles of freedom—of association, of expression, and of movements. Yet, Mr. President, in the case of Seychelles you have in the last years regarded our country simply as a piece of "strategic territory" and totally overlooked the human rights tragedy which has beseeched our peace-loving people as a result of big power geo-politics. Please see herewith attached copy of letter to British Prime Minister, Margaret Thatcher, Secretary General Mikhail Gorbachev and Mr. France A. René of State House, Mahe, Seychelles—all of which are self-explanatory.

On this eve of Christmas 1987, Mr. President, the people of Seychelles pray that your historic Agreement made in the name of common sense with Mr. Mikhail Gorbachev will mark the first step towards the restoration of stability and fraternal understanding in our islands. Any assistance you can bring, Mr. President, towards this noble objective will be greatly appreciated.

Yours sincerely,
James R. Mancham

It was some weeks later that I received the following reply from the United States State Department:

Dear Mr. Mancham,

I have been asked to reply to your letter to the president of December 9, in which you set forth your view of the consequences for Seychelles and United States involvement in the Indian Ocean.

I found your letter and the attached correspondence very interesting. However, I must say that your characterization of our policy toward Seychelles and some of your other assertions are inaccurate.

We do not regard Seychelles as a "strategic territory" but a non-aligned country with whom we have always tried to have cordial relations. Your assumption that the tracking station is the sole driving force behind our relationship is not the case. The station, which is a satellite tracking station and not a "nuclear facility," has existed peacefully on Seychelles for the last twenty-five years, both before and after Seychellois independence.

The U.S. concern for human rights is well-known. Not only do we publish an annual assessment of the human rights situations in many countries, including Seychelles, but we do not hesitate to share our concerns about human rights with any government when warranted.

I am not sure what you mean when you suggest that Seychelles has been the "indirect victim" of U.S.-Soviet rivalry in the Indian Ocean. We have always scrupulously respected Seychelles' non-alignment. Our presence in the Indian Ocean has been to ensure that international shipping routes remain unhindered and that regional stability remains undisturbed.

I note that your letter also contained your congratulations on the signing of the INF treaty, and I am sure that your sentiments were appreciated.

Sincerely
John S. Davison
Director, Office of East African Affairs

Mr. Davison's letter was dated February 4, 1988. It was a good diplomatic exercise which sidestepped several important points, which I had made in my letter to President Reagan. On April 12, 1988, I promptly sent him the following reply:

Dear Mr. Davison,

Thank you for your letter on February 4, 1988, which came to my attention recently following my return to London from a long trip in Australia and Southeast Asia.

Leaving aside the question of whether the U.S. airforce station of Mahé is a nuclear facility or a mere tracking station (you must know it is not easy for a Seychelles islander to tell the difference)—it appears you and your government know or prefer to know very little about the history of this installation.

Ironically, the undersigned himself played a crucial role in the building up of this facility. Soon after Washington, D.C. gave the go-ahead he was retained by both Philco-Ford and Panam Corp. (the two U.S. Companies contracted to build and to run the station on behalf of the U.S. airforce) to look after their interests in the islands. If at the beginning and on the surface, his retainer was to do with his position as a young lawyer, it did not take him long to respond to the call of political dictates for he was known to be overtly pro-West and anti-Communist to the core, and commanded a position of leadership among his innocent people. He has now realized what the CIA, the Pentagon, the State Department, the White House, MI5, Whitehall, and Downing Street already knew, that the day when London and Washington, D.C. agreed to build a U.S. airforce Station on Mahé, was the day when the destabilization of the Seychelles began. As a matter of fact, when a few weeks after this announcement, Mr. France A. René initiated a vicious and vitriolic campaign among the Seychelles people against the

American image generally, and the tracking station in particular, it fell on the undersigned and his supporters to launch a counter-offensive, which began with the people of Seychelles waking up one morning to find their main islands painted with slogans "Yankee, yes—Communism, no"—an offensive carried on for years thereafter in the midst of bomb explosions, arsons, and other civic disturbances aimed at the U.S. presence in the islands. Truly speaking, it does not say much of the mighty United States and its policy that today those who were friends of the United States and who stuck out their necks in the name of freedom and democracy are the ones forced to live in exile ten thousand miles away from home whilst the friends of the Soviets are in full control. My dear Mr. Davison, while to fight with the past can be a complete waste of time, the point remains that the most powerful hurricane cannot shake the foundation of truth.

I note that you have chosen to offer no comment on the allegations I made in my letter to Prime Minister Thatcher about the U.S. build-up in Diego Garcia, and about my question to President Reagan—"Mr. President, don't you think that the moment you built a sophisticated U.S. airforce tracking station on Mahé (which is an island seventeen miles long by four-and-a-half miles wide) and a nuclear naval theater next door, the Seychelles became as much a part of your hemisphere as Grenada?" It is highly hypocritical for the leaders of the "superpowers" to speak about "our hemisphere" when everyday they behave as if the whole world belongs to them.

In your reply you state, "Our presence in the Indian Ocean has been to ensure that international shipping routes remain unhindered and that regional stability remains undisturbed." The stability you speak of must be seen from a Washington standpoint and certainly not from that of the Seychellois people whose forced exile from their beloved islands since René's coup represents on a per capita basis the greatest exodus in the world of a people running away from their homeland for political reasons.

Last but not least, perhaps you could remind President Reagan and Secretary of State Shultz, what I recently reminded Sir Geoffrey Howe, British Secretary of State for Foreign Affairs, that since history has a longterm perspective, the reward of those whose success is based on the ability to manipulate expediency at the expense of fundamental principles can only be *short-term glory*."

In November 1989, I launched the Crusade for Restoration of Democracy in Seychelles. The priority was: (i) to inform and educate world opinion about the Seychelles, (ii) to remind the world leaders that Seychelles was once a democracy but that for the past thirteen years the people of Seychelles had been denied their political freedom, (iii) to provide support and encouragement to the great majority of the people who could not openly express their desire for restoration of democracy for fear of reprisals against themselves and their families, (iv) to demonstrate to the one-party state government that attempts to suppress the desire for political freedom in Seychelles would fail and (v) to promote open political debate with a view of putting in place a government with mandate to govern voted in office on a multiparty basis.

The first achievement of the crusade was the fax revolution it created in the islands.

At that time, there was no free press in the country, so every morning, my associate in the crusade and I would despatch a fax to Seychelles for distribution to the people. They mostly had a revolutionary tone and contents and made the point for early return to multiparty democracy. The faxes were having such an impact on the oppressed people of Seychelles that the one-party state government immediately enacted legislation forbidding anyone to distribute any material received by fax unless such material was related to legitimate company business. One proviso, in fact, compelled the manager of any business to deliver to the security police any fax received which was covered by this legislation. Fortunately, for us, there was another piece of twentieth-century technology which came handy—the photocopying machine. A secretary in an office who was sympathetic to our cause would collect a fax before official office opening, copy it and then hand the original to his or her boss. From one copy of course, a thousand copies were made.

Also as president of the crusade, I started to visit the major capitals of Western nations calling for the return of democracy to Seychelles. I went to Paris, Bonn, Stockholm, Canberra, and Ottawa singing the same song.

On May 15, 1990 I addressed the Heritage Foundation in Washington, D.C.[1] As I addressed the two hundred or so personalities who had been specially invited for the occasion, I could see among the audience, Rear Admiral Robert J. Hanks, who was commander of the United States Middle East force when I was president of the country and who was now senior political-military analyst with the Institute for Foreign Policy Analysis. I told the audience that it was not surprising that at this important juncture in world history, when everybody was clamoring for multiparty democracy, for the Seychelles people to rightfully aspire to a return to freedom in their own islands:

"It would indeed be a sad irony if an interest in protecting Diego Garcia and the U.S. airforce tracking station in the Seychelles should constitute Mr. René's guarantee to continue with his one-party dictatorship and the suppression of the fundamental rights of our people. Mr. René once threatened those installations. Now he holds them hostage. He sees them as his guarantee on power, his insurance policy against any possible change of policy from Washington that might jeopardise his rule."

When I finished my address, there was wide applause and Admiral Hanks was one of those who specially came forward to shake my hands and assured me of his full support for our cause.

---

[1] The Heritage Foundation was established in 1973 as a non-partisan tax exempt policy research Institute dedicated to the principles of free, competitive enterprise, limited government, individual liberty and a strong national defence. The Foundation's research and study programs are designed to make the voices of responsible conservatism heard in Washington D.C., throughout the United States and in the capitals of the world.

# CHAPTER FIFTEEN

# RETURN TO SEYCHELLES

AT THE COMMONWEALTH HEADS OF GOVERNMENT meeting in Harare in September 1991, Secretary General Emeka Anyaoku identified the promotion of democratic practices and human rights in member countries as an emerging priority for the commonwealth in the future. In fact, the one-party state government of Seychelles was put under extreme pressure at this meeting. When the Seychelles delegation returned to Mahé, René announced that multiparty democracy would only come to Seychelles over his dead body. He said that the one-party State had the support of the people and to demonstrate this, he called for district council elections under the aegis of his one-party government. Out of 48,744 people registered, René's candidates had obtained a total of 22,326 votes. There were 6,738 no-votes in the box provided for this purpose. This, therefore, meant some 19,390 people had made a point not to vote despite the pressure they had been put under to do so. Moreover, the 10,000 or so Seychellois who had fled the country since the coup of 1977 and were living overseas had not been given a say in the matter.

I decided that it was timely for me write to René. I thought it would be best to do so on a not-too-formal basis. Thus, I wrote to him on December 1, 1991:

Dear Albert,

I think you must accept that this election does not provide you with any acceptable mandate to create the district councils as a means to perpetuate the one-party system. You know that this election was conducted in an atmosphere void of political opposition. In fact the media, which is under your control, constantly urged the people to go and vote and no one was given the opportunity to argue to the contrary. Your one-party state has become the largest employer in the country and it is a well-known fact that people have lost their jobs for doing much less than voting against your dictate. Furthermore, the election was held under the absolute control and supervision of officials whom you had personally selected.

You see, Albert, in the final analysis, we must be serious about both democracy and national reconciliation if we are to bring about a truly happy Seychelles for ourselves and our children. Indeed, to do so we would have to establish better communication and understanding, which themselves must be built on trust and mutual respect. In the circumstances of today, this will not be easy and will require acts of great statesmanship on our part. I think you should know that it is within the spirit of such statesmanship that I have resisted and continue to resist pressure for us and our supporters, both inside and outside Seychelles, to target the tourism industry as part of our agenda in the struggle for democracy. I believe you are intelligent enough to realize that if I was to relent in this connection, responsible banks would find it very difficult, alone or collectively, to provide you with the $20 million which you are seeking to prop up your bankrupt economy.

In return, can I expect a demonstration of genuine statesmanship on your part, made in the spirit of real national reconciliation, an act from you, which would be sincere and not a bait in which is embedded a vicious hook?

On December 4, 1991, I was again in Washington, D.C. on a lobby mission staying at the Capitol Hilton Hotel when my wife, Catherine, telephoned me from London. She was excited. She said that a fax had come through from René in Seychelles announcing that he was returning the country to multiparty democracy and I could return if I wanted to participate in the process. I asked her to fax to me a copy of René's fax immediately.

Dated December 4, 1991, on the official State House statio-
nery the letter read:

Dear Jim,

Thank you for your letter of December 1, 1991. I am pleased to
attach to this letter a copy of a press release, which was issued
this morning following important decisions taken at the meeting of the congress of the SPPF yesterday to implement a new
constitution for Seychelles based on a pluralistic democratic
system.

You will note from the press release that I have invited all
Seychellois currently residing overseas to return to Seychelles if
they so wish and participate in the political life of the country
in a responsible manner.

I have also urged all Seychellois to forget past divisions and
take a forward-looking approach to the development of our
country in a peaceful environment.

In a statement which I made to the international community this morning, I have stressed that I am ready and willing to
have a dialogue with anyone who wishes to discuss with me any
matter connected with the changes.

A unique opportunity is now available for all of us to forget
our past differences and develop together in a genuinely democratic manner a new constitution which will allow all Seychellois
to participate responsibly in the political life of our country.

The accompanying press release stated that the one-party constitution would be modified at the end of the year to allow registration of political parties. A commission to draw up a new
constitution would be set up in July 1992 on a proportional party
basis aimed at establishing the strength of parties. A group would
have to gain at least five percent of votes to qualify for participation.

That day, I replied to Mr. René as follows:

Dear Albert,

I acknowledge with thanks receipt of your letter of even date
informing me that you have decided to implement a new constitution for Seychelles to restore a pluralistic democratic sys-

tem and forwarding to me a copy of the press release issued by the Seychelles Peoples' Progressive Front.

Your press release brings up several points about the past, about which, I believe, we must agree to disagree if we are to make a fresh start. After all, history has a longterm perspective and at this moment in time we must concentrate on the present and the future.

I welcome your decision to accept the need for multiparty democracy and share your view that a unique opportunity is now available for all of us to work together towards a more stable and happier Seychelles.

Before we can do this, however, there are several points which need to be addressed on an urgent basis. For example, the re-introduction of free speech and access to the media; an acceptable time table under which we move forward in a responsible manner towards multiparty democracy; an end to all intimidation of the opposition; ways and means of reintegrating all Seychellois refugees back into the community. In other words, there is a need for us to sit down and discuss these vital issues and to agree upon the ground rules which would be necessary if the changes envisaged are to be durable and truly democratic.

Accordingly, I propose sending a delegation to Seychelles in the near future to discuss important outstanding issues with you in preparation for my return.

I hope we can work together for a brighter future for the Seychellois people.

On the flight back to London from Washington, D.C., I was thinking a lot about René's decision to return the country to multiparty democracy. For the past fifteen years, I had been living a relatively quiet but happy life in a house on the River Thames where I had made for myself a good name as an international consultant to several business corporations. It was okay to return to Seychelles and play a part in the restoration of democracy but one question was bothering me: "Under what ground rules were we to play?" I could see a situation before me of returning to play on a field which had been demarcated by Mr. René under rules and regulations made by him and with linesmen and a referee also appointed by him. In fact, this is what he was proposing. In the circumstances, I thought that I should not just rush back to Seychelles until I had a clearer picture of what options I had before me. So, I wrote to Mr. René on December 9, 1991 suggesting a meeting on some neutral territory, either Germany or Mauritius, where we could discuss and agree as to what the ground rules would be. I knew that for Mr. René and myself a complex political chess game had begun—but I was afraid that the younger political elements active in Seychelles would not see the nature and dimension of the game and would continue to face developments "horizontally" rather than from an "overview" position.

Thus I organized for Paul Chow to pay a first visit to Seychelles on my behalf. His instruction was to meet the leaders of all opposition factions and to urge them not to get committed to Mr. René's process but to insist that the transition be vested as a responsibility of some recognized and respectable international institution. But Mr. René had seen ahead and put on offer a contribution of 200,000 rupees for each party that would be registered.

Unfortunately, the young political leaders in Seychelles were too eager and enthusiastic to collect the 200,000 rupees. In no time, several groupings had been created under different names, thereby, made themselves available to play on Mr. René's field according to his rules, his supervision and his dictates. Suddenly, it became clear that Mr. René did not need me anymore to be able to bring back democracy or whatever *semblance* of it he had in mind. He had cleverly created enough players to do so in a situation where he could not lose. For myself, therefore, it became a question of either staying in London and being locked out of the transition or return to play on Mr. René's field. I knew that if I returned and played on that field, I could not be heard complaining after the event. But, of course, after fifteen years of living by the Thames, I was longing for some of the warm air and sunshine of the Indian Ocean and I finally made up my mind to return home notwithstanding Mr. René's entrenched advantages.

It was with a sense of high exhilaration that I boarded the British Airways 747 flight at Gatwick airport in the early evening of Saturday, April 11, 1992. I was accompanied by my wife, Catherine, and son, Alexander; as well as some 150 to 200 friends and political associates including Ambassador Walter Carrington, President Carter's former ambassador to Senegal.[1] Ambassador Carrington had come all the way from Washington, D.C. as a representative of the National Democratic Institute in a show of solidarity with our democratic process.

As I boarded the flight, I was reminded of the words of the song sang by my late brother, Mickey:

> *Going back to the Seychelles*
> *Isle of Paradise*
> *A thousand miles from anywhere*
> *In the middle of an ocean*
> *Lies the pearl of the Indian Ocean...*
> *Seychelles, my native land.*

As the plane took off, I remember another historical day in the history of Seychelles when on July 4, 1971, I had boarded a British Airways VC10 in London to be the first passenger to land in the Seychelles on a wide-bodied plane on the opening of our airport. Thousands of people had gathered there to see the "big bird" landing and to express their appreciation for the role I had played to get the airport built. Now, once more, I was returning to the same airport was expecting another big crowd to welcome me. That, in fact, was the case when the next morning on the April 12, I touched Seychelles soil again after nearly sixteen years of life in exile.

As a journalist put it, "...it was the consummation of a love affair between a man and his people." I was afforded a hero's welcome with some ten thousand supporters having gathered at the airport singing *La Paloma Blanca;* which was my favorite song when I was president and which had been banned in Seychelles after the coup.

---

[1] Following his visit to Seychelles, Walter Carrington was appointed by President Clinton to the post of U.S. ambassador in Nigeria.

In the afternoon, I faced the largest rally the country had ever seen—a gathering of over 20,000 people who were in a jubilant and excitable mood. As I glanced at the huge crowd, I knew that most of those who had turned up were, indeed, DP supporters and that the SPPF had stayed at home, except for some curious elements.

With political insight, I could sense that the polarization which had set in, in the early days of politics, was still very much a feature of our political scene. It was obvious to me that the country and the people were eagerly looking forward to changes but it was also obvious that a confrontational approach vis-à-vis Mr. René and the SPPF would only perpetuate the prevailing stalemate. I thought also that, perhaps, the islands were too small for René and Mancham to be at loggerheads. I could understand Mr. René's logic and motivation for wanting to stay in power. I knew that Mr. René was ruthless but that he was also politically astute and has become an excellent manipulator of people.

Finally, I had to face the reality that I was back in the Seychelles, which was still under the control of René's army and that even when I addressed the people, the field on which I stood was under the control of Mr. René's police.

Before I addressed the great crowd, there were also a dozen or two messages to be read to the crowd: two of them came from U.S. congressmen.

One was from Congressman Tom DeLay of Texas which read:

> All the world will be watching the Seychelles in the next few months for signs of real political reform and real change. Your imminent return has not gone unnoticed, defenders of democracy everywhere applaud you for your courage and determination to set your Nation on free once again.
>
> —Tom DeLay, Member of Congress.

The other one was from Congressman Newt Gingrich of the 8th District of Georgia, then Republican Whip and one time, of course, Speaker of the House. Mr. Gingrich's message read:

> The worldwide democratic revolution that began with the crum-

bling of the Berlin Wall in 1989 has, with your return, finally reached the Seychelles.

As the Seychellois prepare to rejoin the free people of the world, it is only appropriate to reflect for a moment on the total failure of the one-party, Socialist state. Seeking to be, rhetorically, all things to all people, the one-party Socialist dictatorship is, in reality, only a vehicle to serve those in power.

I will follow with great interest the progress of the Seychelles on the road to democracy, as will the American people. I wish you and the Seychellois the very best in their soon to be victorious struggle to be free.

—Newt Gingrich, Member of Congress.

Both messages were from Republican congressmen but that was no bother because I had not far from me a smiling Ambassador Carrington representing the National Democratic Institute. All in all, I was glad for the interest mighty America was taking vis-à-vis Little Brother.

Addressing the large crowd, I thanked them for their support and said how nice it was to be on home ground again. Then, I went straight to the point of national reconciliation:

"There is before us," I told them, "an urgent task for this Nation to go through a healing process. For me, national reconciliation is far more important than the position of president itself."

Most of my supporters were exhilarated although there were some who had expected me to lead a riot and later questioned my conciliatory attitude towards Mr. René. The next day at a press conference, I explained:

My attitude towards Mr. René is based on political realism. When President Reagan agreed to meet with President Gorbachev to discuss détente, it was not a matter of soft-heartedness, but the realization that after years of confrontational politics, the leaders of the two superpowers had to meet and dialogue if the Cold War was to end. Now, in the context of Seychelles, I do not see before me any wide-open space to maneuver in the quest for stability, if the main political parties cannot discover the goodwill to put vital long-term national interest before short-term partisan gains. Now I do not see how the SPPF and the DP can bridge the gap if René and I are not on speaking terms.

No doubt, I made it clear to everyone that I had returned to the islands as the Apostle of National Reconciliation.

I knew that things were not going to be easy, that politically, Mr. René had so many entrenched benefits and advantages, which he could manipulate to keep him in power. I also knew that with the wind of free enterprise blowing everywhere, championed by the United States, that eventually things could change for the better in Seychelles.

That is why, I felt so profoundly sad and disappointed when some months later, l was told that the tracking station was going to close down and with it, the U.S. embassy.

# CHAPTER SIXTEEN

# FAREWELL TRACKING STATION

As THE U.S. WAS BUILDING MORE AND MORE FACILITIES in Diego Garcia, American personnel at the tracking station in Seychelles started to indicate that the day was not far off when this station would be closed despite the fact that it had served a very useful role during the Gulf War monitoring military movements over Kuwait, Iraq, and Saudi Arabia.

It was also being mooted that the tracking station in Seychelles had become the most costly one to run within the U.S. satellite system. For Seychelles, the tracking station had, over the years, provided a lucrative rental which had been first agreed around the time of our independence. Later on, after the coup, there had been an agreement for a rental of eight million U.S. dollars a year, which the United States had agreed would be paid under two headings: pure rentals—4.5 million U.S. dollars and the outstanding 3.5 million to be paid under the economic support fund. Under this program, the United States provided the Seychelles with petroleum products, which were then sold to finance development projects in the country. The rental provided a steady flow every year of foreign exchange. And as for the economic support fund project, the agreed practice carried on for several years until Washington came up with the argument that Seychelles had reached too high a GDP to qualify under this vote. In return, the Seychelles government had pointed out that their agreement to receive part of the rental consideration under the economic support fund, was nothing more and nothing less but a desire to meet the U.S. government's own bureaucratic convenience.

There was of course, an agreement based on a difference in the consideration that should be paid except for the foreign exchange shortfall it was bound to create. Nobody would have got specially distressed with the decision to close down the tracking station. After all, Diego Garcia had now come of age, with the most modern technique and technology and what stood on Mahé, Seychelles was no more the latest state-of-the-art technology. However, the simultaneous announcement that once the station would be closed, so would the embassy, was a "hit below the belt" blow to Seychelles.

Immediately, therefore, (October 1995), the government of Seychelles sent her minister of foreign affairs, the late Danielle Jorre de St. Jorre, to Washington, D.C. to plead with the U.S. government to keep the embassy open.

In Washington, D.C., Mrs. Jorre de St. Jorre met with the assistant secretary of the airforce, John Dalton, and argued that the U.S. decision without prior warning to close down the tracking station and the embassy as well as to eradicate the Peace Corps program was most hurting to a country with a fragile economy. She further argued that the financial implications for the United States was only a "drop in the bucket." Dalton replied that the U.S. tracking station had been a valuable asset to the United States, which appreciated the support Seychelles had provided in its thirty-year history. However, in view of major constraints, the decision to close the station had to remain.

After seeing Dalton, Mrs. Jorre de St. Jorre went to the State Department where she met with Mrs. Bushnell, deputy assistant secretary for African Affairs and told her that the United States was dropping the Seychelles "out in the cold" at the most unfortunate time. She pointed out how the Gulf War had eaten up the country's meager foreign exchange reserve by adversely affecting our tourism and by the need created for us to purchase costly fuel on the spot market. Mrs. Bushnell said it was most unfortunate that things had to happen in such sequence. With the embassy closing at the same time as the tracking station, she admitted that the timing was "…surely not positive." In fact, she took the opportunity to confirm that the embassy would be closed by August 1996. She announced that the ambassador in Mauritius would be accredited to the Seychelles and that, "…one or two Seychellois would be appointed to deal with visits and consular issues."

Remembering the days of the beginning of the tracking station, when I was welcomed and feasted in Washington, D.C. by Senator John Tower of Texas, then chairman of the Senate Armed Services Committee, I could not help thinking of the contrast in U.S. behavior with respect to when we were needed as opposed to the new situation.

The decision of the United States to close down the tracking station and the embassy was certainly a big blow not only to the forex in-flow of the small nation but also to the pride and feelings of her people.

This was best reflected in an article, which appeared in the *Seychelles Review* magazine around that time under the heading, "Farewell, Tracking Station":

> The closure of the U.S. tracking station in Seychelles would have had a nonchalant effect had it not also coincided with the decision of the State Department to downgrade their diplomatic representation in Port Victoria to that of a consular agency. Ironically, the day the *Seychelles Nation* announced the closure of this U.S. airforce installation, the Chinese embassy was busy sending out invitations to prominent Seychellois to attend a reception at the Chinese embassy on Friday, September 29, 1995 to commemorate the 46th Anniversary of the founding of the People's Republic of China.
>
> Right from the beginning, the Chinese did not hesitate to buy a prime plot of land and to invest in the building of an embassy that would remain the pride of their people. Sadly, the Americans never did the same—they leased appropriate space at Victoria House, which of course will now be reverted to the owners. As one watches international developments since the end of the so-called Cold War, it is obvious that the Americans have come up as first among equals in the field of military power but the Chinese appear to be winning in the field of real diplo-

macy, at least, in this part of the world.

With Seychelles having an ambassador accredited now for some time to Washington, D.C., the downgrading of the U.S. embassy should have never been the result of a unilateral decision by Big Brother alone. This decision is, to say the least, diplomacy at its worst. Obviously, we must now tell the honorable Marc Marengo[1] that he should downgrade himself from ambassador to consular agent.

At a time when the U.S. is busy building a naval fleet in the Gulf to counteract the growth of so-called Islam fundamentalism emanating from Iran, it is regrettable that Seychelles' strategic dimension has been ignored by the State Department, especially as it is not always easy to determine where the Gulf ends and the Indian Ocean begins.

Over the last few months, Secretary of State Warren Christopher has been busy spelling out that in future U.S. foreign policy would be business, business, business.

It is wondered whether Mr. Christopher was ever notified that the U.S. Heinz Corporation is set to exploit and control the vast tuna potential of this region from a Seychelles headquarters. And what will Mr. Secretary of State Warren Christopher do if tomorrow Enterprise Oil declared that they had discovered a vast reservoir of the precious liquid within Seychelles shores? Perhaps, this would provide the base for an upgrading exercise.

The Seychellois people have survived many years of isolation in the vastness of this huge ocean long before the United States decided to remove the "créoles des iles" from the Chagos Archipelago in order to build the Diego Garcia base.

Now that this base is fully equipped and operational, the existence of the Seychelles can be more or less ignored by American diplomacy. Americans who have come to Seychelles and who love the place are certainly most unhappy about the decision taken by President Clinton's administration. If it is correct that this action is prompted by budgetary constraints, then it must be appreciated for what it is—a penny-wise, pound-foolish decision.

Of course, no nation is able to always give perfect leader-

---

[1] Marc Marengo was the Seychelles ambassador accredited to Washington, D.C. and the United States.

ship. U.S. mass politics, by their nature, are not free of mistakes and of inconsistent decisions. It brings domestic politics into foreign affairs in a nation where the notion of geography and diplomacy remain, unfortunately, very poor.

It is, indeed, an American journalist who wrote, "Gratitude, like love, is never a dependable international emotion."

It is to be noted that after publication of the *Seychelles Review* article, the commander in chief of the United States central command, four-Star general Anthony Zinni, who replaced Desert Storm veteran General Schwarzkopf at the head of the U.S. fifth military constituency, which covers the Middle East, South Asia, and the Indian Ocean paid a visit to Seychelles during which he donated medical equipment worth 1.2 million U.S. dollars from the U.S. government. It was an indication that "Big Brother" was indeed feeling some remorse in the way it has so far behaved towards "Little Brother." Subsequently, General Zinni admitted that Seychelles was the only country in the central command region which did not pose any threat level to the U.S. Navy.

General Zinni's declaration made news in the *Seychelles Review* on October 2000, which reported as follows:

> Giving evidence at a Senate hearing, under the chairmanship of Senator John Warner on the terrorist attack on the USS *Cole* in Yemen, General Anthony Zinni said that twenty-four out of twenty-five countries in the region, under his command, had a terrorist threat level, with which the U.S. navy and Forces had to live with continuously. General Zinni said the only country without a threat level was the Seychelles.
>
> This of course explain the "goodwill" which the U.S. navy has shown towards the Seychelles over recent months. There was first, the consignment of medicine worth $1 million U.S. donated to the Seychelles Medical Department—afterwards the U.S. navy assisted in the dismantling of the Golf ball,[2] which remained standing after the closure of the U.S. airforce tracking station and last but not least was the donation of three out

---

[2]The satellite tracking station looked like a golf ball from an airplane.

of five ex-coastguard vessels worth 2 million U.S. dollars. At the time of the handing over ceremony of the vessels in Port Victoria, Vice-Admiral Charles Moore of the U.S. naval forces central command said they have received request from several navies around the world for these vessels and that following a general assessment, Seychelles was selected to receive the vessels.

According to visiting U.S. Ambassador to Seychelles Mark Erwin the reason for choosing Seychelles was the "strong relationship," which the two countries enjoy.

In light of the importance which the U.S. Navy attaches to a good working relationship with Seychelles, the *Seychelles Review*, once again, made the point that the United States should reopen its embassy in Mahé.

"A little bird in hand is worth many big birds in the bush," was the headline

While the United States has closed down its embassy in Seychelles, Chinese diplomacy was of course taking a different shape. The *Seychelles Nation*—mouthpiece of the government of Seychelles in its issue of December 4, 1998 wrote under the headline—"High Level Chinese Delegation on Official Visit":

The Shenyang municipal government delegation from the People's Republic of China are expected in the country this morning on a two-day official visit. The eleven-strong delegation are being led by H.E., Mr. Mu Suixin, Mayor of the People's Government of Shenyang City. Among the highlights of their visit will be the signing this afternoon of the framework agreement for the Praslin Airport Project. The agreement will be signed on behalf of Seychelles by the Minister for Tourism and Civil Aviation, Ms. Simone de Comarmond and on the Chinese side by the president of the Shenyang Corporation, Mr. Guo Encheng.

During their visit the delegation will also call on the Minister for Industries and International Business, Mr. Joseph Belmont and the Minister for Land Use and Habitat, Mr. Dolor Ernesta. China has provided important grants and concessionary loans to finance major projects in Seychelles. Some of these are the Seychelles Polytechnic, the Roche Caiman swimming pool, the Youth Hostel, the construction of schools, houses, etc.

Most recently, a sixty million rupee (twelve million U.S. dollars) soft loan for the Les Mamelles Housing Redevelopment Project was signed. Seychelles also benefits from Chinese doctors, offers of scholarships in China, coaches in certain sporting disciplines, as well as visits by cultural troupes.

Over recent years, relations between Seychelles and China have been characterized by high-level visits from both sides. Vice-President James Michel has undertaken several landmark visits to Beijing. From China we received Premier Li Peng and Minister of Foreign Affairs Tang Jiaxuan. In June of this year, my wife, myself, and the mayor of Victoria, Mrs. Florence Benstrong, spent ten wonderful days visiting Beijing, Shanghai, and Guanghzou as guests of the Chinese People's Association for Promoting Friendship with Foreigners. The invitation was extended in the context of the celebration of the 25th anniversary of the establishment of diplomatic relations between Seychelles and China.

The Chinese are certainly not in Seychelles for holidays or the purpose of tourism.

# CHAPTER SEVENTEEN

# SOLE SUPERPOWER CANNOT AFFORD TO KEEP ITS EMBASSY

OVER THE YEARS since the establishment of diplomatic relations between the Seychelles and the United States, 10 U.S. Ambassadors have been accredited to the Seychelles. The first three were based in Nairobi, Kenya. Anthony D. Marshall, who presented to me his credentials on July 1, 1976, was a businessman from New York who had a great passion for nature and wildlife. After the coup in 1977, Wilbert John Le Melle presented his credentials to Mr. René on July 19, 1977. Le Melle, who had been an assistant professor of government and research associate was a specialist in African affairs and has written several papers, reports, and studies on Africa. Then there was William Caidwell Harrop, who was at one time director of the Office of Research and Analysis in the State Department and had been deputy assistant secretary of state for African affairs before appointed to the Seychelles position.

David Joseph Fischer was the first American ambassador to reside in Port Victoria. He was accredited on November 2, 1982, and just before his accreditation, President Reagan elevated him to the rank of counsellor in the Senior Foreign Service.

Mr. Irwin Hicks replaced Mr. Fischer on August 31, 1985. A career diplomat for most of his life, Irwin Hicks was serving as deputy executive director in the Bureau of African Affairs in Washington, D.C. before coming to Seychelles.

James E. Moran, who swore allegiance on December 15, 1987, entered the U.S. service in 1952 where he finally held the rank of minister counsellor after a distinguished background of service, which saw him for many years at the State Department. He also occupied posts in Teheran, Moscow, Saigon, and Beijing.

When I returned to Seychelles on April 12, 1992 after years in exile, the first diplomat to welcome me was the U.S. ambassador, Richard Carlson, who had been accredited on October 1, 1991. Two years younger than me, Carlson had an impressive record of service and achievements. I had met him while on a lobby trip to Washington, D.C. where he had just terminated his appointment as director of the *Voice of America* information agency. Mr. Carlson had been director of numerous professional and civic organizations, including the President's council of the Peace Corps. A former commissioner of the San Diego Crime Commission, Carlson was also the recipient of the George Foster Peabody Broadcasting Award for investigative reporting (1975 for KABC-TV, Los Angeles).

When Carlson was recalled to Washington, D.C., he was replaced by Mr. Mack F. Mattingly, a native of the state of Indiana with a very distinguished background of achievements as a Republican leader. From 1981 to 1987, he was the United States senator for the state of Georgia, during which time he was chairman of the military construction sub-committee. From 1987 to 1990, he was assistant secretary for defence support attached to NATO in Brussels. Mattingly had to resign when President Clinton came to power. He was replaced by Mr. Carl Burton Stokes, who was accredited on September 6, 1994. As a black man, Stokes, who had a brother in Congress, had taken many firsts during a distinguished life, which saw him becoming not only the first black mayor of the city of Cleveland, Ohio but also a judge of Cleveland municipal court. In 1973, Simon and Schuster published his political autobiography under the title, *Promises of Power*. This book was republished in 1989 under the title, *Promises of Power—Then and Now*. Carl Stokes fell in love with the Seychelles. He could not believe it when information was received from Washington, D.C. indicating the State Department was thinking of closing its embassy in the Seychelles. On November 8, 1995, while in the U.S., he wrote to me:

...Thank you for reporting my published views on Africa in general, and the Seychelles in particular. I feel very strong about my evaluation of Seychelles' political and economic progress, and its importance to the U.S. That is why I read with great interest the *Seychelles Review* editorial "Farewell Tracking Station." I could not agree with you more! I have seen to it that the editorial has been circulated in the State Depatment, where it is getting good response. It is succinct, balanced, consistent with a progressive foreign policy, wise, and absent of what could be understandable bitterness.

Some months later, ambassador Stokes passed away in Cleveland, Ohio April 3, 1996 where he had gone to receive medical attention.

Those days, the residence of the American ambassadors in Seychelles was a beautiful villa perched on the hill of fashionable Sans Soucis and offered a million-dollar view of the inner islands of the Seychelles archipelago. The villa stood within a large tropical garden from the end of which you could have a great view of Port Victoria and its harbor, particularly with the lights at night. It was the place where Archbishop Makarios of Cyprus had resided while in exile before returning home to lead Cyprus to independence and become its first president. It was certainly a residence fit to accommodate the representative of a great power. I remember going there on several occasions to join Americans on Mahé and their friends celebrate U.S. National Day. After the decision to close the Embassy, this place was sold privately.

And as for the U.S. embassy, from the beginning, it occupied the top floor of Victoria House—which had been, up to now, the most prestigious building in Victoria, standing as it does on State House Avenue. Two floors lower, there was also a large and conspicuous cultural center where one could read most American newspapers and magazines and where one could go and watch CNN and see what you could not see—for political reasons—on our local television network. It was, indeed, a favorite gathering spot for those who thirsted for democracy, for knowledge, and for intellectual growth. After the decision was taken to close down the

---

[1] The tricolor is the blue, white and red national flag of the France.

embassy in Seychelles, the cultural centre became the first casualty. Today, the French have moved into the offices once occupied by the American embassy and there, on top of the building, the Tricolor,[1] has replaced the American flag. What is left today of the American presence in Seychelles is a small office, Room 112, on the first floor of the same Victoria House. On the door, is a signboard denoting that this is the office of the consular agency of the United States of America.

On Wednesday, September 9, 1998, I decided to pay a visit to that office. There, in a small room crammed with books, filing cabinets, a telephone, and a computer or two, with the place looking more like a Caribbean retail shop than a consular agency, stood Patricia Lucy Sinon, an extremely warm and graceful Seychellois lady. Patricia, according to a framed certificate prominently displayed, had been appointed U.S. consular agent on March 13, 1997, the 221st year of the independence of the United States under the authority of Secretary of State, Madeleine Albright. Patricia, who had worked as a secretary at the U.S. embassy in Seychelles under different Ambassadors, had the benefit of attending a three-day consular agency seminar at the National Foreign Affairs Training Center in Washington, D.C. before taking up the position. Today, she takes instructions from the man who is accredited as Seychelles ambassador, Mr. Harold Walter Geisel, who resides more than two thousand miles away on the island of Mauritius where he is also accredited as ambassador. Harold Walter Geisel was deputy assistant secretary of state for information and management and acting chief information officer at the State department before he was made Ambassador to Mauritius and Seychelles. He visits the Seychelles once in a while, mostly coinciding his visit with the arrival in port of a U.S. naval vessel—a reminder of the days of gunboat diplomacy.

In 1997, the USS *Fitzgerald* was in harbor from June 26-30. Ambassador Geisel flew in, and jointly with the officer commanding the *Fitzgerald*, hosted an early National Day reception (that suited him because he could then return to Mauritius to host the National Day reception on its real day). I was glad to go on board and sip a chilled Budweiser, which I had not drank since the closure of the tracking station. That evening I met Ambassador Geisel on board and asked him, "Your Excellency, when do you think we will have a U.S. embassy in Seychelles again?" His reply was spontaneous and to the point, "Mr. Mancham, as soon as you people discover oil, we will be back." Bad diplomacy but pure honesty. Yet how sad an attitude from the world's only superpower!

It is ironic that today the most prominent embassy in Seychelles is that of the People's Republic of China. At the time of our independence, China chose not to lease premises like the United States did but to buy land and build something which would impress. Today on St. Louis Mount overlooking the Port of Victoria where the American company H.J. Heinz has a factory which is canning some 400 tons of tuna a day, the red Chinese flag proudly floats for all to see. There is not one single American flag, which once provided that certain feeling of pride and comfort to American citizens who visited our shores, to be seen in the whole vicinity.

"We are certainly not fair-weather friends. We have come to Seychelles to stay. We do not think it is good policy to close down your embassy just because you have acquired superpower status", a Chinese diplomat put it succinctly.

On November 12, 1998, the *Washington Post* and The *Los Angeles Times* both carried an article entitled "Navy Building Ships over Troubled Waters." It made reference to the visits of United States warships coming to Seychelles for rest and recreation since the closing down of the U.S. embassy and it provided an interesting insight into the diplomacy outlook of Ambassador Geisel, who was quoted as saying, "A lovely thing about ship visits is that they win us friends and they pump money into the economy that is joyfully spent by sailors and marines. It subtly projects our power too. You've got a big goddam ship with guns and helicopters sitting in front of you."

This, Mr. Ambassador, amounts to nothing more but gunboat diplomacy. This is a foreign policy which is based on power and arrogance—and is certainly not consistent with the promotion of friendship and international goodwill.

\* \* \* \*

In March 1999, on a visit to New York City, I founded a Committee for the Restoration of U.S. Diplomatic Presence in Seychelles with the aim of creating more friends for Seychelles within the United States with a view that one day the Republic of Seychelles will have a U.S. ambassador resident again. On that day I wrote to Mr. Harold Geisel, who was representing the United States from Mauritius:

> I am sure that when you were appointed our ambassador with residence in Mauritius, you were presented with a "fait accompli" and had no discretion in the matter. I hope, therefore, it will be possible for you as a friend of Seychelles to support in whatever way you can the noble objectives of the newly formed committee.

I did not receive any acknowledgement of my letter but a few weeks later I was dismayed when I read an article in the *Seychelles Nation* headed, "Attempts to return U.S. Embassy in Victoria—Ambassador Geisel not optimistic."

In fact, this is what the article said:

> Seychelles non-resident U.S. Ambassador H.E. Harold Geisel, who is based in Mauritius, has said he is not optimistic that efforts to return a resident U.S. embassy in Victoria will succeed.
>
> Ambassador Geisel's comment comes in the wake of the setting up by former President James R. Mancham of a committee in New York for the "Restoration of U.S. Diplomatic Presence in Seychelles," as well as a letter sent by Mr. Mancham to the ambassador asking for the latter's full support for the committee.
>
> "I understand and appreciate the patriotic motivations which encourage people in Seychelles to work for the return of a resident U.S. embassy in Victoria although all of us in Port Louis have worked very hard to support the excellent relationship between the United States and Seychelles," Ambassador Geisel said in a statement.
>
> "I would not be honest with my Seychellois friends, however, if I failed to state that I am not optimistic the project will succeed. The same budget pressures that closed our embassy are more intense that ever. Indeed, there is a high-powered committee now at the State Department that is charged with examining the possibility of closing more embassies and replacing them with regional centers similar to what we now have in Port Louis," the statement added.

Disenchanted with the Democratic Party's post-Cold War politics of "Trade and not Aid," I looked forward to the day when a new party would be in power with a more realistic approach to foreign policy.

\* \* \* \*

On January 20, 2001, George W. Bush became the 43rd resident of the United States of America. Some days before, after Vice-President Al Gore had conceded the country's over-timed elections after a split Supreme Court ruled against recounts in contested Florida, I sent a message of congratulations to President Bush. Already in a letter dated January 13, written on paper headed "Bush-Cheney Transition," President-Elect Bush sent me the following reply:

> Dear Sir James:
>
> Thank you for your kind letter of congratulations on my election as President of the United States. I am honored by the choice of the American people and eager to take up the responsibilities of the office.
>
> We will undoubtedly face a number of challenges in the years ahead. I am confident that, with a spirit of mutual respect, cooperation, and open dialogue, we can successfully meet these challenges. The future also presents enormous opportunities. Together we can use these opportunities to advance the peace, freedom, and prosperity of our peoples.
>
> Please accept my best wishes to you and your family for the New Year.
>
> Sincerely,
> George W. Bush

It was indeed a warm and friendly message and clearly indicated that deep at heart, George W. Bush is a good man who wishes well for the American people, and I believe, also the world.

"…the challenges we face…the spirit of mutual respect…cooperation and open dialogue…the opportunities that would come with peace…"—all these were words I wanted to hear and indeed gave me hope for a more caring and sensitive U.S. leadership. Thus on January 31, 2001 from the St. Regis Hotel in Washington, D.C. near the White House, I wrote to General Colin Powell who had become the new secretary of state of the new government:

Dear Mr. Secretary,

I would like first and foremost to congratulate you on your assumption of office as Secretary of State in the Republican Government of President George W. Bush. Mr. Secretary, your recent declaration on the foreign policy of your new administration is a matter which, I know, is being pondered upon by political leaders all over the world. Personally I have come to Washington, D.C. to make the case that your administration considers the reopening of the U.S. embassy in Seychelles because, I believe, you share my view that no country is too small or unimportant if it is surrounded by the sea.

Mr. Secretary, all throughout the Cold War, we in Seychelles agreed to the presence of a U.S. airforce tracking station on our main island of Mahé. One of the main objectives of the station was to gather military intelligence over the former Soviet Union. This having been the case, had there been any physical confrontation within the Soviet Union and the United States we could have been a prime target of destruction by the Soviets. Notwithstanding the aforesaid, Secretary Madeleine Albright of the Clinton administration saw it fit and proper after the Cold War not only to close the satellite tracking station but also the U.S. embassy with it against the argument of budgetary constraints. This "penny-wise, pound foolish" development sent across to our people the questionable message that the United States was only interested in the geography of Seychelles and not in its people. As one who worked closely with the U.S. government and supported the build-up of the tracking station, this unexpected development was most disheartening—coming as it did at a time when we were returning the country to multiparty democracy, so much so, that I wrote a book questioning U.S. behavior under the title of *Oh, Mighty America* (a copy of which is herewith attached).

Mr. Secretary, in a recent issue of the *Seychelles Review* (issue of new year 2000), I have written an article (a copy of which is herewith attached) under the title of "What a Republican Victory in the USA May Mean for Us in Seychelles." While the article is self-explanatory, I would like to quote the paragraph dealing with the terrorist attack on the USS *Cole* in Yemen last year. "Giving evidence at a senate hearing under chairmanship of Senator John Warner on the recent terrorist attack on the USS *Cole* in Yemen, General Anthony Zinni, who collaborated closely with General Colin Powell during the Gulf War and was until recently, commander in chief of central command, said that twenty-four of twenty-five countries in the region under his command had a terrorist threat level, with which the U.S. navy and forces had to live with continuously. General Zinni said that the only country without threat level was the Seychelles. Now, if General Colin Powell does not appreciate that for this reason alone, the Seychelles deserves a U.S. ambassador and embassy in her own right, I do not know who will."

Mr. Secretary of State, you more than anyone in the administration must be aware of the importance of Diego Garcia in your global interest; you must also be aware of the strategic theory that each and every small island can be regarded as an unsinkable aircraft carrier from which missiles could be launched if they were under enemy control; you must also be aware that the U.S. navy often sends ships to Seychelles for rest and recreation and that during this Christmas period a helicopter carrier with over 3,000 navy personnel spent several days in Port Victoria and that more such visits are anticipated. Against this background, can there by any justification for the continued absence of a U.S. ambassador in Victoria, particularly when China, India, France, the United Kingdom and Russia appear to be able to find funds to keep flourishing Embassies?

I believe that the decision by the Clinton administration to close its embassy in Seychelles was not commensurate with an America which constitutes the only superpower in the world today. As a full member of the United Nations, Seychelles votes on all international issues, be it small or big. The decision to close the embassy was a slap in the face to Seychelles sovereignty. This morning in Washington, D.C., I had the opportunity to address a breakfast meeting of the Americans for Tax Reform on this issue after which I was greatly comforted by the rousing ovation and full support I received from all those present. Indeed you can imagine the reaction of American public opinion if an important American citizen be him a senator, congressman, Hollywood personality, or just a business leader having a heart attack on Seychelles soil after disembarking from a cruise ship to find out that there is no U.S. embassy in the country to provide him with any assistance and comfort. This is certainly not in keeping with the image of the new United States about which President Bush and yourself have been speaking.

May I, therefore, be allowed to invite you, Mr. Secretary of State, to rectify as soon as possible the current situation—a decision which, I know, will be greatly welcomed by the government and people of Seychelles as well as Americans of all political persuasions.

Yours sincerely,
Sir James R. Mancham, KBE
Founding President of the Republic of Seychelles

The reply of Secretary of State Powell was short and avoided most of the points I had made:

Dear Sir James,

Thank you for your letter and the copy of your book, *Oh, Mighty America.*

The United States maintains an excellent working relationship with the government of Seychelles. Although resident in Port Louis, Mauritius, our Ambassador, Mark Erwin, understands that there is no substitute for personal contact and has made it a point to travel regularly to Seychelles.

I know we will continue to build upon the close ties our governments have sustained thus far.

Sincerely,
Colin Powell

I had always had the highest regard for General Powell as a man of vision and great stature. I was therefore extremely disappointed with his letter which lacked a touch of enlightened diplomacy and thus did I remain ever determined to continue pressing for the appointment in future of a U.S. ambassador resident in Seychelles because as the secretary of state had himself admitted "…there is no substitute for personal contact."

Meanwhile, Senator Jesse Helms, who was chairman of United States Senate Committee on Foreign Relations wrote to a friend, Mr. Raymond St. Ange who had complained about the absence of a U.S. ambassador in Seychelles: "Thank you for sharing your thoughts on an American Presence Post in Victoria, Seychelles. I support American overseas presence when it serves U.S. national interests and I shall keep a close watch on any senate actions concerning this matter with your views in mind."

Against the background of Congress approval of a 270 billion U.S. dollars Defence Authorities Bill, I found it difficult to accept the argument of closing the embassy in a strategically located country for so-called reasons of "budgetary constraint." If Beijing, London, Moscow, New Delhi and Paris could justify an ambassador for Port Victoria, why not Washington, D.C?

\* \* \* \*

On September 10, 2001, *The Economist Intelligence Unit* of London announced in a newswire country briefing that recent developments suggest that the U.S. administration under President George W. Bush was giving increased strategic significance to Seychelles:

> Recent developments suggest that the U.S. administration under President George W. Bush gives increase strategic significance to Seychelles because of its key position in the Indian Ocean. As part of the exchange program with the United States, thirty officers from the Seychelles people's defence forces took part in a "quality management" seminar in early July, which covered topics such as law enforcement and military operations.
>
> Later in the month, eighteen Seychelles coast guard personnel completed a three-week course under U.S. trainers for "enhancing Seychelles' organic ability to enforce sovereign rights over fishing territories." It was also designed to prepare the Seychelles coast guard service for closer liaison with U.S. vessels in the area.
>
> In addition, the charge d'affaires at the U.S. embassy in Mauritius, Robert Gribben, paid a visit to Seychelles in mid-July and signed grant agreements with a number of NGOs and the self-help program. Talks were also held about sending twenty-five Seychelles Administrators to study in the U.S. under a Programme which benefited thirty-seven Mauritians last year. A planned visit to Victoria by three U.S. navy vessels in late July was reportedly called off, however, because of a terrorist alert in the Middle East.

The day after this news was announced, the terrorists attacked the twin towers in New York City and the Pentagon in Washington, D.C.—and a few days later U.S. navy ships were actively patrolling the Indian Ocean again as part of the U.S. government's readiness for the strike against terror.

A few days later, the U.S. military issued the following notice to all airlines flying over the Indian Ocean:

> 1) Request all civilian and military aircraft contact Diego Garcia Tower prior to reaching 300NM from NKW vortac. Communications with Diego Garcia Tower shall be established via HF on 132B4KH2. If unable on HF, attempt contact on VHF 126.2MHZ or UHF 340.2MHZ. Radio check-in shall include flight number, altitude, origin, destination, and aircraft number.
>
> 2) Request all civilian aircraft remain outside of 300NM from NKW vortac. Commercial and private aircraft flying within 200NM of NKW vortac that demonstrate hostile intent will be subject to being forced down by armed military aircraft.
>
> 3) If necessary, the military has indicated that deadly force will be used to protect this area from unauthorized incursions. The military will use deadly force only as a last resort, after all other means are exhausted.
>
> 4) Official charts outlining airway changes will be made available as soon as possible. In addition, all aircraft operating in this 121.5 MHZ or VHF 243.0MHZ.
>
> 5) It is incumbent on all aviators to know and understand their responsibilities if intercepted. Review aeronautical information manual section 6, 5-6-2 for intercept procedures.

I was on a flight of Air Seychelles from Singapore to Mahé when the captain received the above information. He was quick to assure me that he was on a flight path very much north of Diego Garcia. Nonetheless, he said he had cleared with Diego Garcia particularly as he had sighted two or three bombers much below his flight level cruising fast on the way to destroy targets in Afghanistan.

Indeed the strike against terror was in full swing.

# CHAPTER EIGHTEEN

# DISENCHANTMENT WITH AMERICA'S FOREIGN POLICY

I FIRST STARTED TO BE BOTHERED about the U.S. sole superpower status on January 18, 1997. As a member of the Sheraton President's Club, I had been allocated a suite at their prized property over-looking Frankfurt International Airport. It was a cold, snowy morning. CNN was on and planes from across the Atlantic and, indeed, from all over the world were landing every minute on this prime airport of Germany. I was expected to leave in a few hours on my way to Berlin for a promising business meeting and I should have felt at peace with the world, but somehow, I was struck by an article in the weekend issue of the *International Herald Tribune*. The article was by William Pfaff, the well respected syndicated Columnist of the *Los Angeles Times* and was headed: "Sole Super-power Status Goes to America's Head."

In the article, Pfaff makes reference to a book recently pub-lished in France which records the conversations and confidences of former President François Mitterand during the last moments of his life when he was dying of cancer. "…They are hard those Americans. They are voracious. They want undivided power over the world," Mitterand is supposed to have declared.

For Pfaff, the comment was worth reporting as evidence of a factor in America's relationship to other countries that Americans ordinarily do not acknowledge. Many countries who are political and security allies of Washington at the same time look upon the

United States as a threat to vital national interests or to their national autonomy.

Pfaff elaborated:

> There is, of course, nothing surprising in the tendency of the United States to aggrandize its power and take advantage of it in commerce as well as in political relations. It does so complacently since Americans have always identified the national interest with universal human interests. Confidence in national virtue is what makes the wheel go round in most democracies. However, some recent formulation of American policy and purpose go beyond this...In short, the isolated position of the United States as the sole superpower tending to go to the national head. Congress has acquired the habit of legislating for the world. Cooler spirits in Washington will realize that power naturally generates counterbalancing power, and that however powerful the United States may be, any number of national combinations could become just as powerful or even more powerful, if sufficiently motivated.

I could not help reading Mr. Pfaff's article a second time. Without confidence in national virtue where will any nation find a sustainable resolve to remain great? And if the title to Mr. Pfaff's article was well chosen, how more pertinent and to the point was his concluding advice to fellow Americans.

> One might suggest a rereading of the American realist Hans Morgenthau on the inevitable limits to any nation's power, or George Kennan, when he argues that the permanent influence of a nation comes from its quality, its ability to compel the respect and confidence of a world which despite all its material difficulties, is still more ready to recognize and respect spiritual distinction than material opulence.

For fellow Americans who would find such sentiments too elevated, Pfaff recommends that they read Machiavelli. He has an entire chapter in *The Prince* on why a leader "...must avoid being despised and hated" and about the unpleasant things that happen to a leader who fails to take advice.

A few weeks later, in an article in the *Sunday Times,* entitled "The Dream That Died," Melvyn Bragg, the famous British TV commentator, described how and why, he, who had been in love with America since boyhood days now found its culture infantile and violent. Let me quote from the article where he described the end of the affair:

> Yet, throughout the 1970s as Britain reeled from loss of empire, loss of direction, loss of control in so many areas of life, the lure of the dollar and the land of opportunities still drew us on and there was a sense in which my generation could not really blame America—however much we railed against Cambodia, napalm, South American dictatorship, and, marched on Grosvenor Square[1]...we had taken on America's wounds as tenderly as its aspirations. But when in the 1980s, we were lectured through the movies and through the new triumphalist commentators that "greed was good" and "greed is everything", it was time to say, "That's not us." Greed replaced public service as the ethos. The very words, "public service" became a despised aside...Perhaps, in a quiet way, it is time for us to make our own declaration of independence.

In his last book, *This Noble Land,* the famous American writer, James Michener, described his beloved America thus:

> Within our boundaries, we have almost unimaginable riches—agricultural land capable of providing much of the rest of the world with wheat, corn, beef, and other foods. We have spectacular beauty—our vast prairies, our towering mountains, our deep canyons, our vital rivers. We are a land truly blessed for beneath this beauty lie immense deposits of petroleum and the precious minerals gold and silver.

What Mr. Michener failed to point out is that, despite being a God-fearing nation, the United States today is home to the greatest arms industry the world has ever known—and that through the combined strength of her army, navy, and airforce, she can claim to be the only superpower in the world at the close of this century.

In an article in the *Asian Age* of India dated January 28, 1997 headed "Clinton's America: A Nation the World Can't Do With-

---

[1] Address of U.S. Embassy in London

out," H. Y. Sharada Prasad, commented on the inaugural address which President Clinton had delivered a week before:

The outside world did not figure much in Clinton's speech, which is understandable but one sentence sounds curiously crafted to us who live in marginalized countries. The sentence said "America stands alone as the world's indispensable Nation."

The rest of the world admires America's economic and technological achievements and salutes the strength of American democracy, but the question could still be asked, "What is the need for America to think that it stands alone?"

America is certainly indispensable. Nobody can ignore it or wish it away. But is America alone indispensable? Are other nations "dispensable?"

America's indispensability has been proved time and again in ways big and small—most recently in the manner in which it vetoed for a second term Mr. Boutros Boutros-Ghali as the secretary-general of the United Nations even when the overwhelming majority of Nations were with him."

\* \* \* \*

On July 21, 1998, I flew from Amsterdam to Kilimanjaro in East Africa to attend an international conference on Leadership Challenges of Demilitarization in Africa, which was hosted by the government of the Republic of Tanzania and sponsored by the Arias Foundation for Peace and Human Progress, by the Africa Leadership Forum, and the UNDP (United Nations Development Program).

When I woke up the next morning in Arusha at the Novotel, I could not help feeling in awe of that great undulating landscape around the town which extends for miles and miles towards majestic Mount Kilimanjaro and constitutes one of the greatest safari lands in the world. This is more or less Masai country where this fascinating tribe still lives a nomad life, more or less in harmony with nature and share the space around them with animals of all kinds. It was, I told myself, perhaps the way God must have intended man to live. However, my fascination with the country and the Masai tribe turned into a nightmare when we drove from the hotel to the conference center. The once tarmaced road was badly in need of repair; it was obvious that most of the population around, Arusha was not in any formal employment and that both money and food were scarce. There were no beggars around but it was impossible to make out whether these people were living at the level of apathy, depression, or anger. There was no animosity, but there were also no spontaneous smiles. Yet, this was the Republic of Tanzania of 1998, a country which has known no war and has been run relatively well since it acquired its independence in 1961.

I was impressed by the words of Dr. Oscar Arias, former president of Costa Rica and Nobel Peace Laureate as he delivered his keynote address at the opening of this important conference:

> In the event of war, our global society expresses outrage and immediately works together to stop the flow of bloodshed, but there is a war going on right now that has gone unrecognized yet it is as gruesome as any through the course of human history. Called poverty, disease, ignorance, and injustice, it is the equivalent of a full-scale siege upon our planet's disadvantaged.
>
> Let us recall for only a moment, the horror of Hiroshima— hundreds of thousands of lives, wiped indiscriminately off the face of the earth in one terrible instant. Yet, we would need 236 such bombs to equal today's annual infant mortality rate due to malnutrition.

Every year in the United States, billions are spent in the celebration of Christmas and in Thanksgiving parties. Every year, billions are budgeted for military experiment and expansion and billions are spent for celestial exploration and the conquest of space. Can we continue to ignore these harrowing facts with respect to the people on this planet, Earth?

• There are over 55.5 million refugees in the world and over one-third are found in sub-Saharan Africa.

• Forty thousand children die each day from malnutrition and disease.
• Water contaminated by sewage is estimated to kill two million children every year.
• Furthermore, 293 million people in sub-Saharan Africa alone lack access to any form of sanitation.
• Some 840 million go hungry or face food insecurity.
• Nearly one-third of the people in the least developed countries are not expected to survive to the age of forty
• 1.3 billion people live on incomes of less than one dollar a day.
• 1.5 billion people lack access to health service.
• 1.3 billion people lack access to potable water.
• Nearly one billion are illiterate.

According to the Human Development Report 1998, commissioned by the U.N. Development Program, which was released on Wednesday, September 9, 1998 at the Hague, Netherlands and in more than one hundred other world capitals, fourteen African countries are today trailing the human development Index.

President Clinton's recent visit to some African nations may have provided a glimmer of hope, but surely Africa's colossal problems require more profound and urgent actions—mere words and well-meaning gestures do not suffice. Although aid is desperately needed, Washington's assistance to Africa has dropped to a ten-year low.

Yet, the American economy is in the eighth year of sustained growth that transcends the "German miracle" and the "Japanese miracle" of earlier decades.

According to Mortimer B. Zuckerman who is chairman and editor-in-chief of *U.S. News and World Report*, Publisher of the *New York Daily News* and chairman of Boston Properties:

> Everything that should be up is up—GDP, capital spending, incomes, the stock market, employment, exports, consumer and business confidence. Everything that should be down is down: unemployment, inflation, and interest rates.

In an article in the May/June 1998 issue of *Foreign Affairs*, Zuckerman wrote:

The United States has been ranked number one among major industrial economies for three years in a row. America is riding a capital spending boom that is modernizing its existing industrial base and expanding industrial capacity. The Dow Jones Industrial average is more than four times as high as it was six years ago. The New York and NASDAQ stock exchanges have added over four trillion dollars in value in the last four years alone—the largest single accumulation of wealth in the history of the United States. By contrast, Europe is stagnating and burdened with double-digit unemployment and Asia is floundering in the wake of financial collapse.

There are many explanations for this buoyant, confident mood. One is the get-up-and-go spirit which has always typified America, but surely another is prosperity. This survey of the American economy shows that this is not a transient prosperity but one that derives from a series of structural advantages that today only America enjoys. The rest of the world may improve their public policies through accelerated deregulation and prudent fiscal policy. They may reform their closed and opaque financial systems; they may embrace more fully the technological and logistical revolutions sweeping the business world; they may send their sons and daughters to business schools; they may strive to open up their more parochial business and national cultures. But America will not be standing still. If anything, American business should widen its lead over the rest of the world. France had the seventeenth century, Britain the nineteenth and America the twentieth. It will also have the twenty-first.

But as Dr. Arias puts it:

In the dense rain forests of Central America, Mother Nature frequently provides us with an enlightening lesson. When a storm topples a tree, its roots pull up the roots of the surrounding trees, causing them to fall as well. In much the same way, today's world is a compact forest of cultures, states, and nations whose roots form an interlacing, inextricable network. The survival of each tree depends on the well-being of all the others. A nation traumatized by war, oppression, or poverty is like a tree on the verge of falling. It is an omen of danger for the entire forest.

As I listened to the wise words of Dr. Arias, I was once again reminded of the words of John F. Kennedy whose speeches and declarations had inspired me to become a politician: "If a free society cannot help the many who are poor, it cannot save the few who are rich."

It has been thirty-five years since the fateful Dallas day; the open motorcade, the shot from the book depository, the confusion—and ultimately, the jarring lurch in American history. With conspiracy theories still raging and revisionist historians busy sorting the private man from the popular myth, the true legacy of the John F. Kennedy presidency has been somewhat overshadowed. OK—maybe it wasn't Camelot, but judging by the hold JFK has had on the American psyche, his was presidency that had more than its share of inspirational moments.

On September 11, 1998, the State Department announced that Admiral William Crowe, a former U.S. ambassador to Britain, had been appointed to investigate whether there were security lapses at two U.S. Embassies in Africa hit by suicide bombings on August 7. According to the press release, Crowe was to head two "accountability review boards," which will probe the bombings in Nairobi where 250 people, twelve of them Americans, died and five thousand were injured, and Dar-es-Salaam where ten people were killed and dozens injured. The release also said that the questions they will look into include whether security measures were adequate and properly implemented, what intelligence and information were available and whether anyone was in breach of their duty.

No doubt, the bombing of these two embassies were barbaric actions and all steps should be taken to bring those responsible to justice. But as I thought about that investigation, I felt that it would have been opportune as we were approaching the third millennium, if the president of the United States had also appointed a high-powered committee to look into why there was growing disillusionment with the United States and such gross dislike for some of her policies and to finally make recommendations as to how the United States, as the sole superpower in the world could help to bring about a more equitable world, order of genuine caring and sharing.

\* \* \* \*

On May 25, 2001, I was in New York where I was invited to address the opening banquet of an international symposium on the theme "Serving the Nation—Serving the World", which had been organized by the Interreligious and International Federation for World Peace at the New York Hilton. This is what I said to the over 350 world leaders representing more than 180 Nations at the opening of the Peace Symposium when I was designated as an Ambassador for Peace:

Mr. Chairman, Your Excellencies, Ladies and Gentlemen:

In this world of rapid changes and conflicts towards an unknown future; in this world which has become a global village with men having the ability to ignite it into flame; in this world divided by those who have too much and those who have far too little; where, Mr. Chairman lies the future of humanity, if those of us who are categorized as leaders fail to attend to the urgent task of peace on Earth and goodwill among fellowmen? Where indeed lies the future of humanity if the truth we see and, supposedly seek, cannot be uttered because we have become captive to a situation of prevailing greed, fear, and powerful manipulation.

Everyday, CNN brings home to us the on-going conflicts, the terror of war and destruction against a background of proactive propaganda of hate and divisions. Everyday we see and hear people with a potential for promoting global patriotism, playing to the tune of narrow egoistic nationalism.

Mr. Chairman, I was born on some small islands in the wilderness of a vast ocean at a period when World War II was in full swing. That was in 1939. Today, more than sixty years later, the horror of that war is still being remembered and often brought to screen, although at times one wonders whether beyond short-term commercialism Hollywood does indeed have a commitment to a better world order?

Mr. Chairman, this weekend the great people of the United States of America will be celebrating what they term Memorial Day in memory of those thousands of revered sons and daughters who have fallen victims in one of the great wars involving the United States. Millions across the nation will also, in the name of entertainment, be viewing a dramatized version of a recently released film entitled *Pearl Harbor*. Yet how few in this nation will hear or read about this gathering of ours in New York City today to talk about peace among fellow man, so that there be no Pearl Harbor and no Hiroshima in the future?

Over the years since 1939, war has continued to dominate headlines everywhere. There has been the Korean War and the Vietnam War; the war for the Suez Canal and war in the Northern Ireland; the war in the Congo and the war in Biafra; the Falklands Islands war and the war in Timor; the Bosnian war and the Kosovo war, the war in Afghanistan and the war in Kashmir; the Gulf War. And today, we hear about bombs exploding in Sri Lanka, Macedonia, and the escalation of conflict between Israel and Palestine.

Mr. Chairman, I was born a lively optimist and would hate dying a wretched pessimist. That is why I find great comfort in being here tonight, participating within a cohesion, which, despite all frustration, remains committed to the task of peace and to continued dialogue in search for a better and more equitable world order. I thank the organizers for inviting me again to be here tonight.

Mr. Chairman, machines were invented to be in the service of men. Today men have become slaves of machines—and what is even sadder is that many of us are living like machines—duly programmed to show little feelings and emotions to the ongoing turmoil before us. However, no gun can destroy the voice of the poet of truth and reconciliation, as he calls for peace and reconciliation. It is in this spirit that I want to share with you these few lines which I wrote a few months ago after deeply reflecting about the state of our world today.

> *Come fly with me*
> *I discovered the fruits of my inspiration*
> *In the garden of the moon*
> *Where blue is blue*
> *Red is red*
> *And the flowers which grow*
> *Forever live and never die.*
> *Is this the noble garden of eternity*
> *Staring at me in the face?*

*I see brightness, I see light*
*In the moon of my world*
*The world of my moon*
*Within the constellation of my wandering mind*
*I see the global village I left behind*
*Ceaselessly battling*
*To control the inventions*
*Of its greedy imagination*
*Ushering in a new world order*
*Where laisser faire and laisser vivre*
*Gives way to*
*Let them starve and let them die*
*In the market place of the mighty dollar*
*Where the message that God is great*
*And the father of all*
*Has given way to the motto*
*That might is right*
*So my dear friends*
*Come fly with me*
*To the garden of my moon*
*The moon of my world*
*The world of my moon*
*Where right is might*
*And greed and fear*
*Are forever left behind.*

# CHAPTER NINETEEN

# ON THE EVE OF THE FIGHT AGAINST TERROR

ON SEPTEMBER 14, 2001 I left Seychelles in order to attend a board meeting of a company of which I am a director in Shannon, Ireland. I flew by Air Seychelles from Mahé to Paris where I overnighted before flying to Shannon via London.

That morning I was standing in a queue in front of the Paris Inter-Continental Hotel in Rue Castiglione—waiting for a taxi to take me to Charles de Gaulle, when the hotel porter accosted me and asked whether I would be prepared to share the fare to Charles de Gaulle with a lady who urgently wanted also to get there. I said I would be delighted to oblige.

Mrs. Ruth Silverman was an elderly and distinguished looking Jewish-American lady coming from Bota Racon, Florida. She and a group of friends were vacationing in Tuscany, Italy when they learned about the terrible news of September 11, 2001. While the other friends had decided to complete their holiday plans, she herself was eager to get back home in Florida. She had been ticketed to return to Miami with Air France—but unfortunately at this time, the U.S. Civil Aviation authorities were not allowing foreign registered airplanes to land in the United States. She was therefore going to Charles de Gaulle with a view to have her ticket validated for an American airline flight.

As the taxi speeded along the highway to the Paris airport, I told Mrs. Silverman how much I shared her anguish and pain with respect to what had happened on September 11. Mrs. Silverman was extremely comforted by my remarks.

"Truly I do not know what this hatred of the United States is all about. Personally this is the best country in the world. When my late husband and I got married some fifty years ago, we did not have a penny to our name. But when my husband died last year, he left to me an estate worth nearly two million dollars—and all this money was left for me.

After giving $250,000 to each of our three children, I shared another $500,000 with donations to our synagogue, to a Catholic church and a Methodist ministry—all in the region around our home. I have also made small donations to the Cancer Research Society, the Society for the Prevention of Cruelty to Animals and a lot of other charitable and benevolent organizations and now I am fearful and in tears for what has happened in New York and Washington, D.C. Please, can you tell me once more where you said you come from?"

"The Seychelles," I replied

"Is this the island off the tip of Italy?"

"No," I answered. "What you are referring to is the island of Sicily. The Seychelles is a group of 110 small islands in the middle of the Indian Ocean. For over thirty years we have had a U.S. air force tracking station on our main island. And not far we have Diego Garcia where the United States has the most modern and sophisticated naval and airbase in the world."

"Sorry, I have never heard about your country before."

This made me reflect once again on how ignorant the average American is when it comes to geography—recalling to myself the time when President Reagan welcomed the president of Zambia and asked him how were things in Harare. In fact it was Thomas Jefferson who said, "No people can be both ignorant and free."

With the United States being the only superpower today, it is important that the American people make a point to learn more about the world we live in. Unfortunately, so many know more about the moon than our terrestrial planet. How many, I asked myself, knew about Bagdad before the Gulf War or Kosovo before the war with Yugoslavia?

Suddenly I realized the taxi driver was paying much attention to the ongoing discussions between his two passengers. The driver looked Arabic and I thought it could be interesting to involve him in our conversation.

"Monsieur," I said. "Do you speak English?"

"Enough to be able to follow your discussions—particularly as you are speaking so openly and frankly," he said.

"Well, monsieur—what do you think of the incidents of September 11?"

"Monsieur, I am an Arab and a Muslim. I came to this country from Morocco when I was a young man and over the years I have followed political developments in the Middle East.

First I think that while the Western world has undergone a complete revolution of thoughts in recent centuries, its mistrust of Islam is still essentially medieval.

Monsieur, although Islam has existed for more than 1,500 years, it is still by far the most misunderstood of the great religions of the world. I think this misunderstanding of Islam is at the base of the dislike of Americans vis-à-vis the Arabs."

I interrupted—"I agree that Islam is a great religion—but how do you explain what is going on in Kabul, Afghanistan, where I understand, over one hundred men were recently severely punished for trimming their beards and ninety women for not veiling themselves."

"Monsieur, these are fanatics. They are only a small minority within the Muslim faith."

"Are these fanatics what we consider to be 'fundamentalists'?"

"No, Monsieur, fundamentalists are those people who oppose fellow Muslims who take a more positive view of modernity. Often, fundamentalists begin by withdrawing from mainstream culture to create an enclave of what they describe as 'pure faith.' In fact, their behavior and approach is not unlike the ultra-Orthodox Jewish communities in Jerusalem or New York."

"Do you believe that the ongoing hostilities between Israel and Palestine has anything to do with the attacks on America?"

"Monsieur, I am convinced this is the core of the problem. The Palestinians have got a right to have a state of their own, but this is not possible because of the attitude of Israel. We had Mr. Barak as prime minister of Israel engaged in negotiations with Arafat for a peaceful settlement despite the prevailing hatred and dislike and what do they do? They call Mr. Barak a pacifist and they replace him with Mr. Ariel Sharon, who is perhaps the most militarily aggressive and confrontational leader Israel has ever had.

And then you have President Bush coming into power and distancing the United States from the ongoing problems while providing Israel with military warfare and technology. The Americans may consider the suicide pilots as cowards and beastly people—but from the standpoint of most Arabs, these people were holy fighters, true martyrs."

Suddenly I realized that we had arrived at terminal one of Charles de Gaulle—where I was to be dropped while the taxi would continue with the lady to terminal two. I handed over the fare to the driver together with a tip. The lady wanted to pay half of it. I refused to take her money.

"I would like to meet with you again," she said and then handing a card with her name and a mobile number. She added, "When you are next in Florida, please give me a call. Meanwhile, it has been a pleasure driving with you to the airport. I will make it a point in future to learn more about your country and the Islam faith."

As I got hold of my suitcase to make to the checking counter, I turned back and watched the taxi taking off. I wondered whether the conversation was continuing between the lady from the United States and the French-Moroccan driver—two people whom, I am sure, are good, loving people—yet emotionally torn apart by an on-going turmoil completely beyond their control.

On the flight to London, I reflected on the position of President Bush vis-à-vis the Middle East problem, and above all, about the powerful influence of lobby groups in Washington, D.C., and the way these groups play important roles in influencing and determining U.S. foreign policy—particularly when a group is well funded. As a matter of fact, during the George W. Bush presidential campaign, I was overnighting at the St. Regis Hotel, not far from the White House, on the day when candidate Bush was to address the Jewish lobby. I viewed the whole address from my hotel room as it was beamed live from the Hilton Hotel where the conference was taking place. I was shocked with Mr. Bush's remarks that, if elected, his government would be even more supportive of Israel than that of the Clinton administration.

In fact, at one time during the address, candidate Bush had a long conversation via satellite link with President Barak of Israel during which he gave additional commitments to a more pro-Israeli policy. I was shocked about this because I knew that beyond the shores of the United States, millions of people were already of the opinion that the United States was not being fair minded with respect to the Israel–Palestine equation.

\* \* \* \*

As from Wednesday, September 12, 2001 all national flags in Seychelles were flying at half-mast as a sign of the country's solidarity and expression of condolences to the American people. In a message to President Bush, President René said that the tragic incidents in Washington, D.C. and New York City have left us with a sense of pain, deep shock, and utter disbelief.

On September 13, 2001 I myself wrote to President Bush.

Mr. President:

In this hour of extreme pressure and emotional turmoil, I pray that your resolve be a wise and enlightened one commensurate with your position, not only as president of the United States but also as leader of the most powerful nation in the world.

On Wednesday, September 26, 2001 the Catholic Cathedral of the Immaculate Conception, in our small capital of Victoria was full beyond capacity for an ecumenical service for peace and for the victims of the attacks on America. I was seated in the front row next to the vice-president and cabinet ministers. The Seychelles National Choir was playing "All we are saying, is give peace a chance." It was a colourful and emotional ceremony and at one stage, an American lady, Lucy Luc, who has resided in Seychelles for a long time, turned everyone into tears with her interpretation of *America the Beautiful.* I was particularly taken by the verse:

> *O beautiful for patriot dream*
> *That sees beyond the years*
> *Thine alabaster cities gleam*
> *Undimmed by human tears!*
> *America! America!*
> *God shed his grace on thee*
> *Till nobler men keep once again*
> *Thy whiter jubilee!*

All religious communities in Seychelles were represented including the country's small Islamic society. In a sermon delivered half in French and half in English, Monsignor Denis Wiehe, future Roman Catholic Bishop of Seychelles, quoted Monsignor Rowan Williams the Anglican archbishop of Wales in the United Kingdom who was in Manhattan when the terrorists struck, and who, upon his return to Wales had this to say to his congregation:

Today it is right and proper that we seek for justice. Even in the extremity of anger and misery, people are answerable for the choices they make, and the decisions to kill several thousand innocent people was a real decision, an unspeakably wicked and deluded decision…However, the United States and its allies face a problem and a very real challenge: What is to be done beyond punishment to make any such punishment more than revenge? How do we build something more of a common world of moral reference? How is power to be used so that it is not hated? If, in addition to whatever anti-terrorist measures are taken, the Western governments could make a visible common commitment to some new initiatives that would put power at the service of the most frustrated, what might happen? Perhaps a further round of debt cancellation; or a concerned international initiative to break the deadlock in the Holy Land and to bind the security of Israelis and Palestinians together, or again a review of sanctions in Iraq...In other words, what can be done...alongside the "war on terrorism" which is announced and which is being enacted by the widening international coalition? For...there is no final security without the redistribution of power. And the tragedy is that this is regularly seen as weakness; yet the real weakness is the inability to change the terms of the relation, as if it must always be the terrible drama of contempt and rage...No Christian can accept the political definitions of weakness and strength as they stand.

So here again, as we pray for the victims and their loved ones; as we seek for justice for the thousands of lives so dramatically and brutally terminated on that September morning there is also food for thought and a nagging sense that beyond justice and retaliation, we are called at the same time to change our world view and transform our relationships.

The service ended with a prayer attributed to St. Francis:

> Lord, make us instruments of your peace.
> Where there is hatred, let us sow love;
> Where there is injury, pardon;
> Where there is discord, union;
> Where there is doubt, faith;
> Where there is despair, hope;
> Where there is darkness, light;
> Where there is sadness, joy;
> Grant that we may not so much seek
> to be consoled as to console;
> to be understood as to understand;
> to be loved as to love.
> For it is in giving that we receive;
> it is in pardoning that we are pardoned;
> And it is in dying that we are born to eternal life.

# CHAPTER TWENTY

# ENDURING AND ENSURING FREEDOM

TODAY—TUESDAY, OCTOBER 16, 2001. The local newspaper in Seychelles, the *Nation* carried a leading article on the new Middle East peace push by British Prime Minister Blair and Arafat—alongside another leading article, in bolder headline proclaiming—"U.S. Jets in 'Robust' Strikes as Forth Carrier Nears":

> U.S. warplanes conducted very heavy daylight strikes against troops and other Taliban targets yesterday as a fourth American aircraft carrier move near striking range of Afghanistan, defense officials said…The attacks were robust with about fifty Navy attack jets and as many as ten heavy Air Force B1 and B2 bombers used against military targets including troop concentrations of Afghanistan's ruling Taliban…The Strikes appeared to be the heaviest daylight raids yet in a nine-day-old bombing and missile campaign against Afghanistan's leading Taliban, accused by Washington of harboring fugitive Osama bin Laden, who is suspected of masterminding the September 11 attacks on America…The carrier USS *Theodore Roosevelt*, the carrier USS *Carl Vinson*, the carrier USS *Enterprise*, the carrier USS *Kitty Hawk* are all in the Gulf and Indian Ocean region engaged in the strike against terror…

After reading the local newspaper, I opened up a magazine. It carried several cartoons on the ongoing conflict. One cartoon was in the form of a letter from the Boeing Corporation to Mr. Bin Laden—Dear Mr. Bin Laden—Now that you taken the time to get to know Boeing's fine line of commercial aircraft, we would like to get you acquainted with Boeing's other fine products...." In another cartoon, a journalist was depicted asking the U.S. president—"Mr. President, what evidence you have that the Taliban have sophisticated weapons?" "We have kept the invoices", President Bush is supposed to have replied. And a third cartoon depicted President Bush ordering a U.S. general "Go and blast their tallest building"—which itself was represented by the photo of a three-story high shack.

Well, this is no time for humor. The events of the September 11, 2001 have certainly turned the world upside down and since it is said that there is no ill wind that does not blow anybody good, we must look at the situation with coolheadedness and wisdom as we analyze the situation realistically and take as many lessons from it as we can.

First of all—let us thank heavens that all these jets, carriers, and firepower belongs to the Americans. Just imagine if it was the other way around—goodbye Johnny Walker, goodbye sweet music, goodbye modern civilization—a new world ushered in of men with long untrimmed beards surrounded by ghostly veiled ladies...

* * * *

The question must be asked—who is a terrorist? The best answer I have found for this are the points made by John W. Wood—in an address entitled "Terrorism in a Decade of Disorder," which he delivered at a conference which he chaired in London on December 15, 1993. At that time, Mr. Wood was a director of Oxford Analytica, the Oxford-based policy think tank and the senior fellow of the Center for Security Studies of the University of Hull in United Kingdom—and chairman and founder of the Institute for Applied Science, a non-profit institute dedicated to the prevention of the spread of weapons of mass destruction:

> The question who is a terrorist is, and always will be, open to debate, but one thing we do know is that it is often a relative matter. One man's terrorist is another man's freedom fighter.

Terrorism has operated at some exalted levels. Nuclear deterrence was essentially a terrorist strategy. Winston Churchill said that "...through nuclear deterrence peace would become the sturdy child of terror." This finally led in the closing stages of the Cold War to the esoteric doctrine of mutual assured destruction or MAD. This strange doctrine had its own weird and compelling logic: Terror at guaranteed mutual destruction would ensure there was no destruction. It is important in understanding the mentality of terrorists to appreciate that, in the main, terrorist are not simply psychopaths. People do bad things for reasons that seem good to them. Often today's terrorist is tomorrow's head of state. As Philip Windsor points out, "in mandated Palestine, British troops were subject to terrorist attacks from Arab and Zionist organization alike. Ergun and the Stern gang produced the man who became a Prime Minister of Israel and who then denounced the PLO as a bunch of murderers and thugs." Jomo Kenyatta, after a spell in prison became one of the most respected and stabilizing head of state in Africa. Nelson Mandela will become the president of South Africa. This is merely to say that we must take understanding the mind of the terrorist seriously; it is too easy to write terrorists off as murderous crazies. Many people who are attracted to terrorism are psychopaths. But many are rational decision makers. The threat in general is deeper and more considered than that from mere psychopaths. *Terrorism is the violence and the threat of violence exercised for political effect.* It follows that those that feel they cannot exercise, control in any other way, because they are in an inferior or weak position, will be tempted to turn to terrorism. In fact it has been said that to engage in terrorism is to evidence weakness.

\* \* \* \*

With the end of the Cold War and the collapse of the Soviet Union there had been high hopes that the United States of America, which emerged as the only superpower in the world, would become committed to a better and more equitable world order. This expectation had been fuelled by declarations made by great Americans like the one made by John F. Kennedy when he became president in 1961:

We observe today not a victory of party but a celebration of freedom, symbolizing an end, as well as a beginning, signifying renewal as well as change. Let the word go forth from this time and place, to friend and foe alike, that the torch has been passed to a new generation of Americans…To those new states whom we welcome to the ranks of the free, we pledge our word that one form of colonial control shall not have passed away merely to be replaced by a far more iron tyranny…Let every nation, know whether it wishes us well or ill, that we shall pay any price, bear any burden, meet any hardship, support any friend, oppose any foe, in order to assure the survival and the success of liberty…To those people in the huts and villages across the globe struggling to break the bonds of mass misery, we pledge our best efforts to help them help themselves, for whatever period is required. Not because the Communists may be doing it, not because we seek their votes but because it is right. *If a free society cannot help the many who are poor, it cannot save the few who are rich.*

In fact, during the Cold War the Americans were pro-active in most countries of the world denouncing the evils of communism and promising a better and more equitable world order under their patronage once Communism would have been defeated.

However, when victory came, this was sadly not to be the case. In no time Washington, D.C. had declared that in future its foreign policy was to be based on "Trade" and not "Aids." This was followed by a policy of closing down of embassies—like the one in Seychelles and then emerged a policy of "blackmailing" the U.N. by withholding much needed dues!

It was sad to see emerging a United States which had become forgetful of what President Franklin D. Roosevelt said as early as 1937, two years before I was born. "The test of our progress is not whether we add more to the abundance of those who have much, it is whether we provide enough for those who have too little."

\* \* \* \*

In 1950, Lester Pearson (*Democracy in World Politics*—Princeton University Press. p. 195) warned that humans were moving into "an age when different civilizations will have to learn live side by side in peaceful interchange—learning from each other, studying each other's history and ideals, and art, and culture, mutually enriching each other's lives. The alternative in this over-crowded little world is misunderstanding, clash and catastrophy."

According to Samuel P. Huntington in his book, *The Clash of Civilizations and the Remarking of World Order* (Simon & Schuster, p.303):

> The overriding lesson of the history of civilizations, however, is that many things are probable but nothing is inevitable. Civilizations can and have reformed and renewed themselves. The central issue for the West is whether, quite apart from any external challenges, it is capable of stopping and reversing the internal process of decay. Can the West renew itself or will sustained internal rot simply accelerate its end and/or subordination to other economically and demographically more dynamic civilizations?

In conclusion, Huntington whose book was described as "…dazzling in its scope and grasp of the intricacies of contemporary global politics" by Francis Fukuyama of the *Wall Street Journal*, states,

> In the emerging era, clashes of civilizations are the greatest threat to world peace and an international order based on civilizations is the surest safeguard against world war.

In his most recently published book, *Does America need a Foreign Policy?—Towards a Diplomacy for the 21ˢᵗ Century* (Simon & Schuster. Copyright 2001), America's most celebrated diplomatist Henry Kessinger concludes:

> Whilst traditional patterns are in transition and the very basis of experience and knowledge is being revolutionized, America's ultimate challenge is to transform its power into moral consensus, promoting its values not by imposition but by their willing acceptance in a world that, for all its seeming resistence, desperately needs enlightened leadership.

Yes, I do know that at this moment there is no appetite in the United States for anything which could sound conniving of terrorism. But blind patriotism cannot be the answer to a better and more secured future. The American people as a whole must be educated beyond the breaking news of their many television stations. Washington, D.C. has a duty to govern and administer the nation in accordance with the traditional sentiments and values of the American people. It is wrong for the good people of America to be manipulated to support policies, which in the end bring them into hatred, ridicule, and conflict on the international stage. This amounts to a betrayal of the trust the people put into their leaders.

In this moment of national reflection, I believe that my American friends should accept the cause of my disenchantment, because while I support the drive of the United States to eradicate terrorism, it is also my very firm conviction that we will not enter a better world order without strong and truly dedicated U.S. moral leadership. Without this, we will continue to live in a global village of increasing disorder and decadence.

# CHAPTER TWENTY-ONE

# THE FUTURE

On September 4, 2001 I received an invitation from the Summit Council for World Peace to attend Assembly 2001, sponsored by the Interreligious and International Federation for World Peace (IIFWP) and dedicated to the theme "A New Vision of Leadership: The Search for Solutions to Critical Global Problems" that was to be held from October 19 to 22, in New York City.

In the aftermath of the dreadful events of September 11, 2001, I enquired from the organizers whether the conference was still to take place. The response was prompt. "It is now more than ever— necessary to hold Assembly 2001, which is dedicated to building bridges of cooperation and peace among the nations, races, nationalities, cultures and religions that make our global society"— Mr. William Selig an Executive Officer of the IIFWP, assured me by fax. Today as a designated Ambassador for Peace, I considered myself most fortunate to have over the last few years participated in the various conferences organized by IIFWP since all of them have proactively resolved that all the religions of the world must unite within the framework of an inter-faith cohesion that will ensure that religion is not a source of strife but a basis for lasting peace.

On Friday October 19, at the New York Hilton Hotel, I addressed the 600 delegates representing 110 Nations all of whom are members of today's global village. While making clear that I supported the United States' rights to seek justice for what happened on September 11, 2001, I nonetheless criticized Washington's post-Cold War foreign policy, which abruptly became based on "Trade" and not "Aids" and which was then followed by a policy of closing down the embassies like the one in Seychelles and then the policy of withholding much needed U.N. dues. I indeed emphasized that it was my very deep conviction that U.S. moral leadership was essential for a better world order.

There were indeed some remarkable speeches and remarks from some of today's great thinkers, philosophers, politicians and men of God, from not only the United States, but also across the world, made at the conference. Some arguments at time became heated and controversial—but there was an element of depth and considerable soul searching in all of them.

"America's leaders must develop patience in their efforts to extract justice. Peace cannot be secured within our borders while relentlessly and aggressively pursuing the Prince of Darkness. Destroying precious resources and killing countless innocent lives, while hunting down and killing Osama bin Laden, will not bring terrorism to a screeching hault! Such a pursuit would only multiply the darkness because it would fuel the fires of aggression and hate. We must not find pleasure in killing the flesh, but healing the spirit that have given way to savagery," declared the most reverend George Augustus Stallings, Jr., D.D. in a most fiery and well-crafted address reminiscent of the famous Mark Anthony's speech of ancient Roman times.

"Let no one be deceived and make no mistake about it: On Tuesday September 11, hate killed, not religion! Whether unjustifiable in the eyes of some or justifiable in the eyes of those who deemed their acts at righteous indignation, the reality is "hate killed", the fiery Archbishop declared to audience-wide applause.

Reverend George Augustus Stallings is the archbishop of the autonomous, independent and African-centered Catholic Church, known as Imani Temple, which is headquartered in Washington, D.C. He is a member of the executive committee of the World Bishop's Council and chairman of the executive committee of the American Clergy Leadership Conference, an interreligious, interfaith, and interracial coalition of ministers throughout the United

States of America.

In conclusion, Archbishop Stallings addressed his people, the American people, about the need to bring more spirituality in the area of U.S. foreign policy:

> ...When all has been said and done, let our legacy, as a people and global community, be to future generations that there existed a people who, despite all odds, led the world with a love of God and humanity. They conquered evil by refusing to be seduced by hatred and revenge. And, for that reason, we as a people shall forever be called God's people, a peculiar people, a chosen generation, a royal priesthood, a holy nation that God has set apart to bring about world peace. There can be no peace without justice. No justice, no peace. The reality is that, as people of the world, we will not be able to change the course of foreign policy and bring about global peace until we look deep down within ourselves and become peacemakers in our own hearts...

According to Mr. Norman G. Kurland, president of the Center for Economic and Social Justice, Israel and Palestine should fuse together with "...special trade status in the global market place" to form the "Abraham Federation." This, according to him, constitutes a new framework for peace in the Middle East:

> Many nations are offering their solutions to end Israeli occupation of the West Bank. None of these initiatives seems to be satisfactory to both side of the conflict. In that light, the Abraham Federation concept might well offer a new framework for those directly affected to recapture the initiative, not merely for their own survival, but for leading all mankind to a more just and peaceful future.

Mr. Kurland's proposal for such a federation was originally published in *World Citizen News* in December 1978 and re-published in *America-Arab Affairs* in spring 1991.

I was, of course, looking forward to the remarks of my longstanding friend Arnaud de Borchgrave, whom I befriended some thirty years ago when, following the Seychelles coup in 1977, he interviewed me for *Newsweek* in his capacity of chief foreign correspondent of that magazine. Since then, he has co-authored with Robert Moss the best-selling novel *The Spike*, which drew on his extensive knowledge of Soviet KGB operations. From 1985 to 1991 he was editor-in-chief of the *Washington Times* and of *Insight* magazine. Today he is editor-at-large for the United Press International (UPI) and the *Washington Times.*

Throughout his fifty-five years of covering wars, revolutions, assassinations, and other major world crisis, Mr. de Borchgrave has developed a "tell-it-like-it-is" approach which has seemingly provided him with a license to be blunt and undiplomatic:

> ...Transnational terrorism is a hydra-headed snake that feeds on perceived injustices and inequities suffered by the developing world at the hands of an uncaring capitalist world. The United States and its allies now have a historic opportunity to give the demagogues of the Muslim world the lie by dusting off a speech George C. Marshall gave at Harvard in 1947. Bin Laden believes he found the answer to a superpower's overwhelming military power by waging asymmetrical warfare. But his terrorist swamp would quickly drain when faced with a Western new deal, such as debt forgiveness, for the poor nations of what we once called the Third World.
>
> Ever bigger defense budgets are not the answer. The September 11th tragedy has given the United States and its western allies an unexpected opening to turn adversity into a geopolitical victory. New approaches to development in developing world must be on a scale that I witnessed and covered as a journalist, that put Europe back on its feet and on the road to prosperity after World War II.
>
> As long as we have two billion people, one third of humanity, struggling to subsist on $2 a day or less, we will have spawning grounds for transnational terrorism carried out by people who have nothing to lose..."

Mr. Gordon L. Anderson, secretary general of the Professors World Peace Academy who earned his master in divinity in Christian Ethics at Union Theology Seminary and his Ph.D. in Philosophy of Religion from the Claremont Graduate School could not, because of time constraints, deliver his long and well-researched address on leadership and governance in the twenty-first century in full, but in his précis of it, his message came loud and clear:

...We have entered a global age and have witnessed global terrorism, anarchy, and moral relativism. History has brought us
to the point where we have to recognize that we all share one
world together and that the actions of one can affect everyone
else. At all levels of society, we must overcome selfishness, nationalism and other "isms." Global structures should genuinely
represent the entire world's people if they are to be perceived as
legitimate...

In a global community, nations must overcome nationalism and genuinely serve all of their people. Because of global-
ization, people from many cultural and ethnic backgrounds must
coexist under one government, a modern government must allow freedom for these people to claim their own cultural background while pursuing happiness. Under freedom, today's
stateless and marginalized people can create new homes. The
United Nations and other global institutions should encourage
the adoption of human rights and freedoms in countries where
they are lacking. These changes may not be easy or come quickly,
but they are possible. The sooner we collectively work on constructive reforms, the brighter the future will be for a world of
peace and justice for our children.

So far as the Dr. Kennedy Simmonds who was head of the
government of St. Kitts and Nevis in the Caribbean from 1980 to
1985 is concerned, the global crisis we face today is being fuelled
by ignorance, callousness for human life, injustice, and an un-
healthy lust for power over the minds of our young people:

...We the people, in families, in communities small and large,
across the global landscape must examine ourselves, our preju-
dices, and our thought processes to see how we can better work
with others to determine what aspects of development and what
practices in our society are negatively influencing our youth.
Then forge a coalition with the youth, the religions, the media,
the governments, and all civic organizations to develop and
implement a constructive agenda to rebuild our communities
upon the principles of equity, justice and inclusiveness...

For Mr. Antonio L. Betancourt, executive director of The Summit Council for World Peace and president of World Institute for
Development of Peace and deputy secretary-general of The Fed-

eration for World Peace, there is today a need for a new awakening within civil society, first between religions, and then between religions and state in order to promote true justice that balances the purpose of the individual with the purpose of the whole to achieve true peace and prosperity:

> …The nations of the world, especially the Unites States, which has been recognized by historians and philosophers as a nation with a manifest destiny, need to consider today how much of their founding ideals and values are reflected in their modern everyday culture, education, economic policy, foreign policy, etc. Nations need deep reflection because there are often great contradictions between the thought of their founding fathers and their modern thinking, practices and national policy.
>
> For example, in the United States, the moral and spiritual values that were espoused by its founding fathers and which gave birth to the great documents that embody the American ideal are challenged today by a modern intellectual elite that is at best agnostic and cynical towards religion and moral values, and at worst hostile towards religion and morality.

Others who spoke at this conference included Dan Quayle, former vice president of the United States; H.E. Abdurahman Wahid, former President of Indonesia; H.E. Jose de Venecia Jr., Speaker of the House, Philippines; the Hon. Lloyd E. Sandiford, former prime minister of Barbados; Hon. Minister Louis Farrakhan of the nation of Islam; Dr Frank Kaufman, Director of the World Peace Institute; Mr. Taj Hamad, international executive Director of the World Association of Non-Governmental Organizations; Rabbi David Broadman, chief rabbi of the city of Savion, Israel; Mr. David Caprara, president of the America Family Coalition; Rev. Hunsei Terasawa, leading Buddhist Monk of Japan; H.E. Stanislav Shuskevich, former president of Belarus; Rt. Hon, Edward Schreyer, former governor general of Canada; Dr. Neil Salonen, president of the University of Bridgeport; Hon. Richard Thornburg, former U.S. attorney general; Hon. Danny K. Davis, U.S. congressman (Illinois); Hon. Larry Pressler, Former U.S. senator (South Dakota) and Mr. Thomas Walsh, currently secretary-general of the IIFWP, Rev. Dr. Chung Hwan Kwak, Chairman of

IIFWP, and Dr. Nicholas N. Kittrie, Chairman of the Eleanor
Roosevelt Institute of Justice and Peace.

I had met most of these personalities over the last three years
at diverse conferences sponsored by the IIFWP in Seoul, Washington, D.C. and New York City and had become impressed with
the need for an active cultivation of a culture of peace.

\* \* \* \*

I was first introduced to Grover Norquist some 20 years ago when
I went to Washington D.C. to lobby for support for the return of
the Seychelles to multi-party democracy. At that time he had just
returned from visiting anti-communist nucleus operating in far-
away Nations and in war zones on the Pakistan and Afghanistan
borders. In no time, this stocky bearded Harvard's-educated intellectual had assured me of his total support for the Crusade for the
restoration of democracy in Seychelles, which I had, together with
a friend, Paul Chow, launched in London.

Subsequently, after the USA closed down its Embassy in
Seychelles Grover became very supportive of my actions and initiatives to have it re-opened.

For many years now, Grover Norquist has been President for
Tax Reform, an organization of over 90,000 individuals, Tax Payers, Advocacy Groups, Corporations and Associations that are
deeply concerned with the high level of taxation and Government's
spending.

However, despite his heavy commitments with this group he
was always ready to help and assist me organize a meaningful and
effective program whenever I was to visit the U.S. Capital. On
two or three occasions I met with Newt Gingrich, Speaker of the
House of Representatives. On another occasion I addressed the
Heritage Foundation. On several occasions I spoke at the National
Press Club. All the programs he organized included a courtesy call
on the Jewish lobby.

One afternoon after a hectic morning of meetings, feeling somewhat jet-lagged, I enquired whether it was necessary that we keep

an appointment with the Jewish lobby since we did not have any Jews or Arabs in Seychelles.

Grover was quick to retort, "My friend you do not get very far in this City, if you pass through it, without paying your respect to this lobby group."

Over recent years Grover Norquist organized regular meetings in a room next to his office in L Street in Washington D.C. on a Wednesday, which is known today as the "Wednesday Meeting." Norquist, the power and idea broker, chaired over usually a hundred individuals representing Conservative activists, Congressional staffers and think-tank analysts who had come from all over the Nation. I always therefore timed any visit to Washington D.C. to include a Wednesday, as Grover would always afford me a few minutes to plead the Seychelles cause. Normally at the end of my address, I would receive some applause and a few up and coming young Republicans would converge towards me with words of encouragements and support. At these meetings I learned a lot about the USA and the way the two party's political game was being played. I was also amazed at the little time given to serious discussions of Foreign Policy issues—particularly when a Presidential election campaign was on the horizon.

I remember well one of the meetings I attended during Governor George W. Bush's campaign for the Presidency. When I walked into the room there was already about one hundred individuals, men and women, helping themselves to either coffee or tea and a bagel or doughnut. Grover walked in at 8.30 A.M. sharp and business was on. It started with him making some comments on some issues of current interest and then the floor took over. The first to step forward was a Conservative-attired fellow from Seattle in the State of Washington D.C.

He announced his name and looking straight at Grover Norquist said words more or less to this effect. "Mr. Chairman, last week I notified this committee that I had been chosen as a candidate of the Republican Party for the State of Washington D.C. for the forth-coming elections and appealed to the committee for some campaign funds and promotional support. I was asked to return to the committee this week listing ten positive points about my Democratic Party opponent as well as ten of his most negative points. Mr. Chairman, here are the ten good points and the ten bad points."

After the fellow had finished reading the "balance sheet" concerning his democratic opponent, Grover Norquist's ruling was prompt and up to the point.

"Thank you for turning up. We shall help you in your campaign by totally forgetting the ten positive points about your opponent and launch a campaign that will put under the microscope the last four negative points. Please make contact soon."

The fellow replied, "I am most grateful to you Sir."

Then came a fellow who had attended a pro-gun lobby conference from somewhere in Arizona.… Then there was someone reporting on an address made during the weekend by Hillary Clinton.… Then Grover called on me to say my few words knowing that I had another meeting to attend at the office of The Foundation for Democracy in Africa.

As I sat in the taxi, moving towards The Foundation, I could not help questioning the quality of democracy in the USA itself. I felt a sense of uneasiness with the growing confrontational approach to party politics which, I considered, to be "un-healthy" in so far as the interest of this mighty nation was concerned. The prevailing policy of ruthlessness and polarization was in my view breeding un-necessary hate and dissension within the nation.

On the afternoon of the September 26, 2001, President George W. Bush met with fifteen prominent Muslim and Arab-Americans at the White House—a visit which has been adversely commented upon by liberal publications such as the *Boston Phoenix* and the *New Republic* alleging that Grover Norquist had brought "terrorism sympathizers" to the White House. In this connection, it is interesting to note that not even his fierce critics were charging that Norquist is anti-Semitic or opposed to the U.S. policy in the Middle East. As a matter of fact, in his book *Rock the House* Norquist argued that "supporters of Israel" are an important part of the Republican Party Conservative coalition.

"He has done an enormous amount to bring the voice of Jews into politics," Rabbi Daniel Lapin, President of the politically conservative Jewish group Towards Tradition told *Insight* magazine on the day Norquist was honored with its "Toward A New Alliance" Award.

Grover Norquist has denied all allegations that he has micromanaged the "specifics" of any White House meetings but admitted, "I have been a long time advocate of outreach to the Muslims community."

On this issue, perhaps our American friends should read what the well-respected United Kingdom's political commentator, William Rees-Mogg said in the conclusion of his article "How could one man get it all so wrong?" which appeared in a mid-November 2001 issue of the *Sunday Times* of London.

> The West needs to make a new political approach. Inevitably oil has distorted the relationship between Islam and the West. Most significant Islamic countries of the Middle East are not those which have most oil, but those which have the most developed societies, particularly the larger countries. Perhaps most important are the three large Arab countries of Egypt, Syria and Iraq and three adjoining non-Arab countries of Turkey, Iran and Pakistan.
>
> The present relationships between the West and these countries differ widely, ranging through good relations with Turkey and Egypt, manageable relations with Pakistan and Syria, to the damaged relations with Iran and hostile relations with Iraq. When bin Laden is gone, Islam will remain a problem and an opportunity for the world. A new friendship should be sought with the large Islamic powers. Globalism without Islam will make no sense.

\* \* \* \*

Before September 11, 2001, New York's Mayor Rudolf W. Giuliani was undoubtedly a popular figure in his great City. After September 11, Giuliani became internationally famous for the way he handled the affairs of his City—perhaps the greatest Metropolis in the world, after it had been viciously attacked in what the United

States considered "an unprovoked act of war." The attack resulted in the demise of some thousands of men and women from 80 different Nations.

When the United Nations General Assembly 2001 opened for its annual debates, Mayor Giuliani was invited to address it. It was the first time since 1951 that a Mayor of New York had addressed the U.N. General Assembly.

"The attack is a direct assault of the founding principles of the United Nations itself," Mayor Giuliani declared.

He said the determination resolve and leadership of the President of the United States, George W. Bush had unified American and descent men and women around the world. The strength of the United States response followed the principles for which it stood. Americans are not of one race or religion, but had emerged from all nations.

"It is our belief in religious, political and economic freedom, in democracy, rule of law and respect for human rights, which made us American and which made New York—'the shining City on a hill.' No city or country had seen more immigrants in less time than New York and the United States, who sought freedom, opportunity and decency. Each Nations in the Assembly had contributed citizens to the United States and New York. In each land there were many who were Americans in spirit by virtue of shared principles. It is perverse that because of these principles we find ourselves under attack by terrorists," the Mayor declared.

I watched the whole address in a hotel room in London, touched, impressed and endeared with Mayor Giuliani's choice of words and overall performance, sharing the view of millions in the world who regarded his actions and commitments after the collapse of the Twin Towers as exceptional. He certainly came up as a leader who was able to remain cool and level-headed under pressure.

However, I must admit that I was not one who applauded Mayor Giuliani's rejection of the $10 million donation to the Twin Towers Fund which Prince Alwaleed bin Talal bin Abdul Aziz Alsaud of Saudi Arabia had made because he had called upon the American Government to pursue a more balanced Middle East policy in future.

On the 12ᵗʰ of October 2001, *The New York Times* carried an article by Jennifer Steinhauer under heading "A Nation Challenged: The Donations; Citing Comments on Attack, Giuliani Rejects Saudi's Gift."

According to this article, Prince Alwaleed had been one of the foreign visitors who accompanied the Mayor to ground zero. After that, he gave the Mayor a check for $10 million for the Twin Towers Fund, a charity set up by Mr. Giuliani primarily for survivors of uniformed workers who died. Mr. Giuliani initially accepted the check, which was accompanied by a letter from the Prince in which he expressed his condolences for "the lost of life that the City of New York has suffered."

His letter continued. "I would also like to condemn all forms of terrorism, and in doing so, I am reiterating Saudi Arabia's strong stands against these tragic and horrendous acts."

However, according to Jennifer Steinhauer the letter did not say what a news release attached to a copy of the letter did: "However, at times like this one, we must address some of the issues that led to such a criminal attack. I believe the Government of the United States of America should re-examine its policies in the Middle East and adopt a more balanced stance towards the Palestinian cause."

Admitting that New York has a huge Jewish population, was it justifiable for the mayor to slight the prince for projecting a perception which is generally held by most people beyond the borders of the United States and the State of Israel?

I have known Prince Alwaleed since I invited his father, Prince Talal bin Abdul Aziz Alsaud, to visit the Seychelles in the early 1970s with a view to get him to support a yacht marina development. Today, Prince Alwaleed is a private entrepreneur and international investor. His father Prince Talal is a brother of the King of Saudi Arabia and his grandfather, King Abdulaziz was in fact the founder of the Kingdom of Saudi Arabia. His maternal grandfather, Mr. Riadh El-Solh was the first Prime Minister of modern day Lebanon.

Prince Alwaleed was born in 1957 (the year that I, as a young 17 years old, who was making my way to London from Seychelles to study Law). Prince Alwaleed earned his Bachelor of Science Degree in Business Administration *magna cum laude* from Menlo College in California in 1979. In 1985 he received a Master's Degree in Social Science, with Honors, from Syracuse University in New York. In 1992, in recognition of his business and academic achievements, he was awarded a Doctorate of Humane Letters, *honoris causa*, from the University of New Haven in Connecticut.

While I was living in political exile in Europe I met with Prince Alwaleed on several occasions in Southern France where he spent a considerable part of his summer vacation each year cruising the Mediterranean on his father's yacht which was usually berthed in Cannes.

The last time I saw him was in July 1997 when he came to Seychelles for a day's visit. I met him at the airport and escorted him around our main Island. During the hours together we talked about each and everything. When he left I had no doubt in my mind that the prince had a lot of time for things American.

Jennifer Steinhauer's article in the *The New York Times* was followed by another article also in *The New York Times* on October 16, 2001 which attacked the prince. The article by Thomas L. Friedman was entitled "Foreign Affairs; Saudi Royals and Reality."

...No doubt there is deep Arab anger over U.S. support for Israel. I've gotten angry myself over the failure of successive U.S. governments to restrain Israel's voracious settlement-building program. But to suggest that Israel is slaughtering Palestinians for sport, as if a war were not going on there, which Israel did not court, in which civilians on both sides are being killed—or to suggest that President Clinton didn't spend the whole end of his term forging a real plan for a Palestinian state, which Yasir Arafat ran away from, with the Saudi government only a few steps behind him, because it required some fair compromises on Jerusalem – or to suggest that somehow Arab anger over any of this, justified people blowing up buildings in New York – is just a lie.... If you really want to honor the terrorists' victims, Prince Alwaleed, set up a newspaper and TV station in Saudi

Arabia—not in London—that can freely publish such thoughts. Then we'll start to feel that the roots of this tragedy are being addressed."

On the 31ˢᵗ October 2001, *The New York Times* allowed the Prince to state his position and published the following article by him.

Like thousands of my fellow Saudis, I studied in the United States, do business with American companies and have a great affection for New York City. Being educated in New York has given me a deep respect for the city and its people, many of whom I count as friends.

I came to New York on October 11 out of concern for people who are dear to me and to share their grief and trauma resulting from the criminal acts of September 11.

I am deeply concerned that this tragedy has opened a rift between our two peoples, partly because some of the hijackers were Saudi citizens. In Saudi Arabia, we were shocked to learn that some of our countrymen could commit such an atrocity.

I can understand why my proposed $10 million gift to the Twin Towers Fund and subsequent statement on American foreign policy has stirred a mixture of sentiments. Americans are experiencing a new suspicion of Saudi Arabia; because this suspicion is utterly unwarranted, many Saudis are questioning the depth of America's friendship with our country.

My message is clear and constant: Saudi-American relations are vital, strategic and built on a legacy of shared interests. My friendship with Americans will survive this controversy; my pro-American sentiments cannot be shaken. A decade ago, America came to our assistance to deter the terrorism of Saddam Hussein. We cannot forget that sacrifice, and we shall always remain grateful.

With regard to the terrorist acts of Sept. 11, I reject the notion that any person or any cause can justify terrorism. The Sept. 11 attacks will never be justified. Period!

I have long sought to bridge the gap between views of people from the Middle East, especially Saudis, and those of Americans. As someone who cares deeply about the relationship, it is my duty to help my American friends focus on efforts that prevent rifts between our countries.

To this end, Americans and Saudis must address some

longstanding issues. For decades now, Arabs have been focused on the seemingly intractable Palestinian-Israeli conflict, and they sincerely want it resolved as soon as possible. It is this view that I have tried to communicate in some of my comments.

What I had hoped to accomplish, and still hope to achieve, is a closing of gaps between our countries so that we can stand united against the horror of terrorism and build a secure and just peace for all the peoples of the Middle East.

I am glad to see that the American administration has been actively supporting a permanent solution to the Middle East crisis. President Bush has stated his desire to see the establishment of a Palestinian State. Secretary of State Colin Powell has reiterated this view. Arabs welcome such statements coming from the American Administration as a light at the end of a long and dark tunnel. I believe we all want, together, to get out of the dark.

No doubt the Prince must have realized that in no way could he perpetuate a fight against mighty America and had decided to react in an enlightened and cool manner, but is it too much for Mayor Giuliani and New Yorkers to be reminded that Prince Alwaleed is the investor who in 1991 attracted worldwide attention when he invested approximately $800 million into the rescue of Citicorp, making him the largest shareholder of the largest bank in the USA. This investment was made at a time when business analysts were predicting the collapse of Citicorp.

In 1993, Prince Alwaleed made a strategic investment of $100 million in Saks Fifth Avenue, the New York fashion retailer, in which he owns approximately a 10 percent interest.

In July 1994, Prince Alwaleed announced a strategic investment in the Fairmont Hotel Chains in San Francisco forming an equal partnership with the original Fairmont owners to position the Fairmont for aggressive growth.

In October 1994, Prince Alwaleed again attracted international attention when he agreed to acquire up to 24 percent of the Disneyland Resort and Theme Park near Paris for more than $345 million.

In November 1994, the same Prince Alwaleed agreed with the founder and controlling shareholder of the Four Seasons Regent

Hotel Resort, the luxury hotel chains, to acquire 25 percent for more than $120 million.

In June 1995, Prince Alwaleed acquired 42 percent of the New York Plaza Hotel and in September 1996 he purchased a 40 percent stake in its sister hotel the 379 room Copley Plazza in Boston.

In July 1995, Prince Alwaleed achieved a new success by taking a stake of 3 prrcent of Mediaset S.P.A. an Italian subsidiary of Fininvest Group for more than $100 million.

In October 1995, Prince Alwaleed, jointly with a group of Americans and other investors gained control of Canary Wharf, the largest real estate development project in Europe. The deal was for $1.2 billion.

In December 1996, Prince Alwaleed purchased the Hotel George V in Paris for $181 million. The hotel is one of the most prestigious in the world having recently re-established its former glory through a major renovations program.

In March 1997, Prince Alwaleed marked a new beginning in his investment strategy by entering the Airline Industry. He acquired a 5 percent stake in Trans World Airlines for $21 million.

These investments are over and above the massive commitments which his company, Kingdom Corporation, has in the field of banking, industry, telecommunications, and hotels development in Saudi Arabia and many other Middle East countries.

New Yorkers are certainly not a naïve people. Many must indeed appreciate the sort of stuff which Prince Alwaleed is made of. Many too must also have admired the confidence he displayed in New York's stability and well-being by the massive investments he put into their city before September 11, 2001.

Over recent days, I have often wondered how many of my American friends—New Yorkers, Texans, Californians and all—have had the opportunity to read the book written by Andrew and Leslie Cockburn, entitled, *Dangerous Liason* and subtitled, *The Inside Story of the US-Israeli Covert Relationship and the International Activities It has Served to Conceal* (London: The Bodley Head, March 1991).

An excerpt from the book which is reproduced on its back-cover states:

> Once upon a time Israel needed powerful allies in an unfriendly Washington, and it found them at the CIA. The young country had pitifully few resources to trade, but it did have the loyalty of Jews behind the Iron Curtain who could be put to work on behalf of American intelligence. For the cold warriors at Langley this was a precious asset, and they were prepared to be generous in return. As the struggle between East and West spread to cover the entire Third World, the secret agencies of the two countries found that there was much business they could do together, business that had better not be done in the open, or ever talked about...

The book cover also mention the praise given to it:

> Should stand for a long time as the alpha and omega of the relationship between the United States and Israel.
> —*Chicago Tribune.*

> A gem of clarity...meticulously documented, and damming as hell.
> —*Village Voice*

> Full of astonishing revelations... *Dangerous Liaison* demonstrates a seriousness and credibility which is not usually shown by books on secrets services.
> —*Ha'aretz* (Israel)

\* \* \* \*

In the democratic world, governments are supposed to be merely an external manifestation of the will of the people. That is why it has become important for the civil society to espouse a new set of values based on interreligious harmony, true justice, human rights, and the full recognition of fundamental freedom as the pillars on which true societies should be built in this century.

It is against this background that one should recognize the value of the efforts deployed by the Reverend Sun Myung Moon since he founded The Interreligious and International Federation for World Peace and the Summit Council for World Peace in 1981. Over the last twenty years, these organizations have been active assembling heads of states, former heads of states, prime ministers, former prime ministers, religious leaders, academics, and media people—all with a view to promote a culture of peace in an otherwise sadly divided world:

> A peaceful nation is needed before there can be world peace. The pre-condition for peace in a nation is peace in the family. Power, wealth, and knowledge, which worldly people have ordinarily desired, cannot be the necessary condition for peace and happiness. True happiness is not proportional to how much property one owns, and is not dependent on the external degree of comfort. Genuine peace and infinite happiness can only be gained when we serve others with true love, and when that love is returned…

This is the core of the message which the most Reverend Sun Myung Moon has consistently propounded over the last twenty years all over the world in gatherings and assemblies sponsored by the Interreligious and International Federation for World Peace.

In November 2000, I was informed by Mr. K.D. Pillay, chairman of the Indian Ocean Chapter of the Rajiv Gandhi Foundation that I had been nominated to be included in the United Nations list of Goodwill Ambassadors. Mr. Pillay attached copy of a letter his organization had sent to Mr. Kofi Annan, Secretary General of the United Nations.

The letter read:

Dear Sir,

Re: Re-nomination of Sir James R. Mancham, KBE to be included in the United Nations list as a Goodwill Ambassador

We are a non-governmental organization (NGO) functioning in Seychelles. Our organization was inaugurated by Mrs. Sonia Gandhi (Chairperson, R.G.F., New Delhi) in 1996. The R.G.F., (IOC) covers the Indian Ocean islands (Mauritius, Madagascar, Seychelles, and Réunion). Our activities are mainly in the field of education, health, environment, and promotion for peace.

Recently, it has come to our knowledge that you have inaugurated a forum with more than forty world celebrities as members. In that line, we believe that the former president of the Republic of Seychelles, Sir James R. Mancham, KBE, is an appropriate person to add to your list of Goodwill Ambassadors. Since his return to Seychelles in 1992, Sir James has been active promoting peace and reconciliation within the country. He is at the moment serving on the Advisory of the Foundation for Democracy in Africa; The Free Africa Foundation; The Summit Council for World Peace and he is also on the list of Arbiters of World Intellectual Property Organisation (WIPO). We are attaching herewith a more detailed profile of Sir James and his background

At this time when the world has become a global village, we believe it would be appropriate for our region to be represented within your list of Goodwill Ambassadors.

We kindly request you to consider our proposal.

No doubt I was deeply moved that my personal interest in a peaceful world was being heard and recognized. As a matter of fact, at the AfriCando 2000 Conference, which took place in Miami, Florida, (May 16 to 19, 2000), the Washington, D.C.-based Foundation for Democracy in Africa presented me with a trophy saluting "Your promotion of peace, reconciliation and prosperity in Africa." This recognition deeply went to my heart as I realized that I had a duty against the basis of my privileged experience and background, to contribute my share in the search of a better world order.

You can, therefore, imagine my happiness and enthusiasm when in early 2001 I was asked to become an ambassador for peace within a movement which Reverend Moon had initiated to constitute a worldwide network of leaders from a wide range of fields, religious, politics, the media, academia, and civil society, to work cooperatively for the sake of world peace. In fact under the auspices of the Interreligious and International Federation for World Peace seminars had been organized all over the world for this purpose. The positive reaction of leaders everywhere was manisfest evidence of a profound interest in the development of a comprehensive international and interreligious approach to peace. I believe that for this initiative alone Reverend Sun Myung Moon fully qualifies for the Nobel Peace Prize.

\* \* \* \*

This year's Nobel Peace Prize was awarded to the United Nations and its Secretary-General Mr. Kofi Annan. Coming in the aftermath of the September 11, 2001 and at the height of the strike against terror, it was evident that the Nobel Prize Committee wanted to emphasize the value they place on the United Nations in the area of international security and conflict.

Free nations, especially the United States and the rest of the developed world have based their economic and foreign policies on social Darwinism "survival of the fittest." This means that weak peoples and nations have been left to die because only the strongest will make it. According to Mr. Antonio Betancourt, Executive director of the Summit Council for World Peace.

"This may be good for the animal world but not for humanity. The developed world must conduct their economic and foreign policies not based on narrow nationalism or 'self-interest.' They have to work together with the rest of the community of nations in the interest of all without a zero-sum gain in which the advancement of one is at the expense of the other."

In this connection, it is imperative that the leading governments of the free world exercise proper leadership roles and give full support in order that the United Nations becomes a respectful and effective body.

The United Nations came into being against a background of what came to be known as the Atlantic Charter when on August 14, 1941, President Franklin Delano Roosevelt of the United States and Prime Minister Winston Churchill of the United Kingdom signed a document on the ship HMS *Prince of Wales* "somewhere at sea," which proposed a set of principles for international collaboration in maintaining peace and security. Some six months later, on June 1, 1942, representatives of twenty-six nations who had been allies in World War II met in Washington, D.C. to pledge their support for the Atlantic Charter by signing the "Declaration by United Nations." This document contained the first official use of the term of "United Nations," which had been suggested by President Roosevelt.

In a document signed in Moscow on October 30, 1943, the government of the Soviet Union, the United Kingdom, the United States, and China called for an early establishment of an international organization to maintain peace and security. The goal was reaffirmed at the meeting of the leaders of the United States, the USSR, and the United Kingdom, at Tehran on December 1, 1943.

The blueprint of the United Nations was prepared at a conference held at a mansion known as Dombarton Oaks in Washington, D.C. During two phases of meetings, which run from September 21 through October 7, 1944, the United States, the USSR, and China agreed on the aims, structure, and functioning of a world organization.

About six months later, February 11, 1945, following a meeting in Yalta, President Roosevelt, Prime Minister Churchill and Premier Joseph Stalin declared their resolve to establish "A general international organistion to maintain peace and security."

On April 25, 1945, delegates of fifty nations met in San Francisco for the United Nations Conference on International Organization. The delegates drew up the 111-article charter, which was adopted unanimously on June 25, 1945 in the San Francisco Opera House. The next day, they signed it in the Herbst Theater auditorium of the Veterans War Memorial Building.

The United Nations was in fact created against the background of the devastations created by World War II which killed over sixty million people and destroyed many great cities.

Let us not forget the words of Harry Truman as he addressed the world in San Francisco on the day the U.N. charter was adopted:

> If we fail to use the charter and the organization that we have created with it, we shall betray all those who have died in order

that we might meet here in freedom and in safety to create it. If we seek to use it selfishly for the advantage of one nation or small groups of nations, we shall be equally guilty of that betrayal. But what a great day in history this can be. This charter is no more perfect than our own constitution but like the constitution it must be made to live. The powerful nations must accept the responsibility for leadership towards a world of peace.

This was not the commitment of a party or of a person. This was the commitment of a nation which had, in the circumstances, become the leader of the international community.

To mark the United Nations Millennium Assembly, Kamalesh Sharma of Park Avenue, New York edited a collection of great essays from contributors who were invited to imagine tomorrow, letting their imagination stretch and rethink a future they would like to see realize on the main global challenges. The collection was published under the title *Imagining Tomorrow—Rethinking the Global Challenge*.

Perhaps the most important and relevant essay contributed was the one by William J. Vanden Heuvel, who was deputy U.S. permanent representative to the U.N. from 1979 to 1981:

> …The founding of the United Nations incorporated the lessons that we had learned from two terrible wars in this century, foremost the lesson that peace can only be secured if the nations of the world, accepting the responsibility of collective security, work together to resist aggression. We understood that the self-determination of nations and peoples was part of the fabric of justice that we had to create in this world. We knew that we had to have an organization that insisted on respect for human rights, that encouraged economic and social and cultural and humanitarian cooperation among the nations of the world. In 1945, with the founding of the United Nations, we had an organization that was dedicated to the very essence of what we as a nation stood for—the four freedoms that Franklin Roosevelt had enunciated—freedom of speech and expression, freedom of worship, freedom from want, freedom from fear—words incorporated in the charter of the United Nations itself. And every nation in the world was signatory to that charter. Here was a document, a charter for the world, which the United States had

such a dramatic and visionary role in creating. It was our opportunity and our responsibility to carry that charter forward. What we were saying was not that the world was perfect, but we knew the world that we wanted and the world that each of us were going to work to create; and through the grace of God we had the nations of the world committed to that same objective. What an extraordinary moment in human history. We took great pride in this achievement as Americans. What greater accomplishment could we have hoped for?

Vanden Heuvel also writes about the U.N. bashers of the last decade:

> …The United Nations is not a perfect organization, but its critics have set up an impossible norm demanding of the United Nations what no government on this earth has ever achieved, perfection in administration and operations. The United Nations has responded over and over again to every demand of the United States, especially in the financial area. The congress said we want control over the budget, that we would not be subject to a general assembly where a majority vote can spend American money. The general assembly now adopts a budget only by consensus, which means that the United States has a veto over it. We demanded that the United Nations reorganize its budget and administrative framework—and said we want an American in charge. The U.N. accepted the demand. Then the Unied States demanded an inspector general, and unless the U.N. put an inspector general in place, the United States was not going to pay its dues. The U.N. put in an inspector general. An outstanding European was appointed as inspector general and given total independence in his action. What does the congress do? It continued to refuse to pay its dues. So every time the congress puts the goal post in place and the United Nations comes up to it, it moves the goal post. These are not forces that are trying to make the United Nations effective. These are forces that are trying to undermine the United Nations. There is no point talking serious reform with people who really are intent on destroying the United Nations.

In conclusion, Vanden Heuvel calls on the president of the United States to educate the American people about the U.N. and to provide it with all the support it deserves:

...And we Americans also have to suggest to our president that he cannot avoid his responsibility for speaking for the United Nations and explaining to the American people what the U.N. is, what the U.N. does and why it serves America's interests. Every president before has done it, and President Clinton and his successor must do it. The polls show sixty-seven percent of the American people want a strong and effective United Nations and want the United States to lead it. Whether we are Democrats or Republican, each of us have to get out there and fight for something that on our agenda is crucial and important, namely, the honoring of America's international commitments and the support and leadership of an effective U.N. The United Nations is the only machinery we have for collective cooperation among nations, the only global tool that we have for promoting peace, security, and protecting human rights and strengthening international law. If the United Nations fails, the United States fails. And if it is a failure, it is our failure. Our task is to lead, to work together as Americans to make the U.N. effective, and when we criticize it, to do so in such a way that will make the United Nations stronger and more effective. The founding fathers of the United Nations were our presidents and our leaders. It is their vision which is our legacy and our trust. Not their politics but their purpose must unify us behind the U.N. once more.

\* \* \* \*

On Tuesday, September 21, 1976, Seychelles was accepted by acclamation as the 145th member of the United Nations.

On that occasion I was privileged to address the opening session of the 1976 General Assembly.

...I think the time has come when we must ask ourselves what will make the world a sane world. The answer is only sane people. What will make the world peaceful? The answer is only peaceful people. For too long the strange notion has persisted in human beings that a state of sanity and peace can somehow be produced by arms struggle and violence. That the end justifies the means is a lie which has been swallowed by almost everyone. It would be much more accurate to say that the end reveals the means.

We do not have to look very far or very closely to see that there are simple and natural laws which work as surely in human affairs as they do in the rest of creation. If you sow a mango seed you get a mango tree. If you sow maize you get maize. No exception to this simple law has ever occurred or ever will. By the same token if you sow the seed of contention, violence and hatred the harvest will be more violence, and more hatred. Society can only change by first changing the attitude of people who live in it and the world can only change by changing the attitude of the nations who constitute it...

At the moment there is a total of forty-two member states of the U.N. that fall under the category of small Islands out of a total of 189 members. These island states take their membership in the United Nations very seriously because of the many vulnerabilities which surround them and their survival.

Unfortunately, island nations are never fully in control of their destiny because their geographic location can render them to become "of strategic interest" in the competing arena of bigger and more powerful nations.

Small island nations are mostly fragile and delicate and, therefore, need to pursue a policy of balanced development and strict conservation. Nonetheless, they can still suddenly found themselves victims of major environmental disasters beyond their control. Like the recent oil spill off the Galapagos when a tanker carrying about 243,000 gallons of fuel ran aground and began leaking diesel oil, destroying tortoises and rare species of birds and plants.

There is the problem of global warming, which according to a report issued at the Shanghai Conference, pictured a world not far in the future when so many small island nations, especially the low-lying islands of coral formations, would be adversely affected by the consequence of an ever-rising tide.

The prime economy of several island nations have over the last few generations been based on the success of their hotels and tourism industry. There is today a great menace. In the short-term by the events of September 11, 2001 and its ongoing consequences and in the long-term by the increasing number of cruise ships and floating hotels which are being built. As a Caribbean friend recently told me, "Our American visitors today come ashore for only four P's—to buy some postcards, to take some photos, to drink a Pepsi, and to have a pee."

In order to counteract against the decline of the tourism receipts, many leaders of island nations have succumbed to the urge and arguments of lawyers from the United States and Europe to turn their country into tax havens and to introduce offshore banking systems—only to be blamed ultimately by the bigger and more prosperous nations to have become protective of their mafias and as well as becoming money-laundering centers.

Under the law of the Sea Convention, several island nations have economic jurisdiction over areas of oil and mineral deposits still to be discovered and exploited as well as rich fishing grounds. But as I pointed out in a conference held in Seoul last year (2000), "As long as your island produces coconut oil, its internal peace and cohesion will not be disturbed but beware the day you discover the real stuff. "

Most islands constitute living laboratories of successful multiracial living which in a world plagued by tribalism, Communism and racism is no mean achievement.

In fact, international law has conferred the privilege of sovereignty, which has given each island nation the right to speak and vote on international issues, be they big or small. Unfortunately, there is in this area the politics of "sphere of influence" within which we see important decisions taken more often for immediate regional consideration rather than long-term global interest.

For the above reasons, it is only reasonable to expect small island nations to support the need of a respected and effective United Nations, as part and parcel of an effective and respected world order. In today's global village, the United States of America should entertain diplomatic relations at an ambassadorial level with all members of the United Nations if only out of a policy of respect and support for the U.N. body. Certainly U.S. Secretary of State Colin Powell, whose descendants were Jamaican immigrants, should be able to appreciate the sensitive side of this issue.

We should all finally realize that the fundamental response to any world crisis must be based on the consensus of universally shared values on John Donne's premise that "…no man is an Island just unto himself—we are all part of the whole."

\* \* \* \*

On the November 16, 2001, the Seychelles Permanent Representative to the United Nations, Ambassador Claude Morel also had his say at U.N. General Assembly debate. After going through various points of introductory averments, Ambassador Morel concluded.

> "…As a small island state whose economy depends mainly on tourism and related industries, Seychelles' vulnerability is obviously at stake, should the on-going military campaign in Afghanistan persist.
>
> As a peaceful community enjoying stability and social harmony, Seychelles, without questioning its strong moral support to the cause of international security, also encourages a dialogue giving the voices of reason and compassion a chance to be heard. Especially with regards to the needs of the Afghan people who have lived three decades of war, resulting in the suffering of very large numbers of refugees and displaced persons.
>
> Mr. President,
>
> Finally, Seychelles would like to lay stress on the urgency for the United Nations to rethink the world order not just in terms of geo-political balance but in terms of a new ethic. International terrorism cannot be fought by way of offensive weapons, either traditional or sophisticated.
>
> To agree on a common value system is in the middle and long term a more profitable orientation for the whole humanity.
>
> This being said, Seychelles renews its adhesion to the international coalition of nations that are united in the war on international terrorism and in the quest for worldwide peace and security."

I was glad that our Ambassador was given the opportunity to state our Government's views on the on-going conflict. After all, as I reminded U.S. Secretary of State Colin Powell in my letter urging him to re-open the U.S. Embassy in Seychelles, no country is too small if it surrounded by the sea. Indeed in the global village of today, there is no reason as to why the voice from Seychelles should remain just "a voice in the wilderness."

And for those who prefers sports to politics, let me proudly announce that just a few day before Ambassador Morel spoke at the United Nations, a group of girls from Seychelles (country with population of 80,000) won the 13th African Volleyball Nations Cup at Port Harcourt, Nigeria where they first took South Africa (country with population of over 60 million) to the cleaners in their first game winning all three sets; they then defeated Nigeria (country with population of over 115 million) on their home ground 3-2, before finally knocking out Cameroon (country with population of over 14 million) to become winners of the 13th African Volleyball Nations Cup for the year 2001.

\* \* \* \*

While the United States enjoyed rapid economic growth during the past 20 years, many poor countries including some of the world's poorest in sub-Saharan Africa, had a generation experiencing an outright decline in living standards. Private consumption spending per capita rose by 1.9 percent per year during 1980 to 1998 in the United States, whilst declining on average by 1.2 percent per year in Sub-Saharan Africa.

In a special report published this year by *The Washington Quarterly* on behalf of The Centre for Strategic and International Studies and the Massachusetts Institute of Technology—Jeffrey D. Sachs who is Director of the Centre for International development and Galen L. Stone Professor of International Trade in the Department of Economics at Harvard asked, "Is there a 'strategic significance' to global inequalities in income levels and economic growth, and if so, which policies might the United States pursue to address those strategic concerns?"

According to Professor Sachs, focusing on the scope and limitations of U.S. foreign assistance as a policy instrument to address global income inequalities is illuminating

> The economic success of developing countries enhances the well-being of the United States, which has and should more actively deploy policy instruments to help support economic success abroad. National interests in successful economic growth abroad are multifaceted. Some of these interests are basically economic: the economic success or failure of developing countries determines the gains from trade and investment that the United States reaps in its economic relations with those countries. The ramifications for the United States, however, of good or bad economic performance among the poor countries go beyond direct economic returns. As a general proposition, economic failure abroad raises the risk of State failure as well. When foreign States malfunction, in the sense that they fail to provide public goods for their populations, their societies are likely to experience steeply escalating problems that spill over to the rest of the world, including the United States. Failed States are seedbeds of violence, terrorism, international criminality, mass migration and refugee movements, drug trafficking, and disease.

The most important speech delivered at the 56th Session of the United Nations General Assembly 2001 was without any doubt that of the President of the United States of America, George W. Bush. It was a speech heard by a worldwide audience.

After making varying remarks to justify the on-going strike against terror, this is how President Bush concluded his address.

> …In this world, there are good causes and bad causes, and we may disagree on where that line is drawn. Yet, there is no such thing as a good terrorist. No national aspiration, no remembered wrong can ever justify the deliberate murder of the innocent. Any government that rejects this principle, trying to pick and choose its terrorist friends, will know the consequences.
>
> We must speak the truth about terror. Let us never tolerate outrageous conspiracy theories concerning the attacks of September 11, malicious lies that attempt to shift the blame away from the terrorists themselves, away from the guilty. To inflame ethnic hatred is to advance the cause of terror.
>
> The war against terror must not serve as an excuse to perse-

cute ethnic and religious minorities in any country. Innocent people must be allowed to live their own lives, by their own customs, under their own religion.

And every nation must have avenues for the peaceful expression of opinion and dissent. When these avenues are closed, the temptation to speak through violence grows.

We must press on with our agenda for peace and prosperity in every land.

My country has pledged to encouraging development and expanding trade. My country had pledged to investing in education and combating AIDS and other infectious diseases around the world.

Following Sept. 11, these pledges are even more important. In our struggle against hateful groups that exploit poverty and despair, we must offer an alternative of opportunity and hope.

The American government also stands by its commitment to a just peace in the Middle East. We are working toward the day when two states—Israel and Palestine—live peacefully together within secure and recognized borders as called for by the Security Council resolutions.

We will do all in our power to bring both parties back into negotiations. But peace will only come when all have sworn off forever incitement, violence and terror.

And finally, this struggle is a defining moment for the United Nations itself. And the world needs its principled leadership. It undermines the credibility of this great institution, for example, when the Commission on Human Rights offers seats to the world's most persistent violators of human rights. The United Nations depends above all on its moral authority and that authority must be preserved.

The steps I've described will not be easy. For all nations, they will require effort. For some nations, they will require great courage. Yet, the cost of inaction is far greater. The only alternative to victory is a nightmare world, where every city is a potential killing field.

As I've told the American people, freedom and fear are at war. We face enemies that hate not our policies but our existence, the tolerance of openness and creative culture that defines us. But the outcome of this conflict is certain. There is a current in history, and it runs toward freedom.

Our enemies resent it and dismiss it, but the dreams of mankind are defined by liberty, the natural right to create and build and worship and live in dignity. When men and women are released from oppression and isolation, they find fulfillment and hope, and they leave poverty by the millions.

These aspirations are lifting up the peoples of Europe, Asia, Africa and the Americas, and they can lift up all of the Islamic world. We stand for the permanent hopes of humanity, and those hopes will not be denied.

We are confident too, that history has an author who fills time and eternity with is purpose. We know that evil is real, but good will prevail against it. This is the teaching of many faiths.

And in that assurance, we gain strength for a long journey. It is our task, the task of this generation, to provide the response to aggression and terror. We have no other choice, because there is no other peace.

We did not ask for this mission, yet there is honor in history's call. We have a chance to write the story or our times, a story of courage defeating cruelty and light overcoming darkness. This calling is worthy of any life and worthy of every nation. So let us go forward, confident, determined and unafraid.

"An alternative of opportunity and hope…" "a just peace in the Middle East…" "principled leadership of the United Nations…" "There is a current in history and it runs toward freedom…" "the dreams of mankind are defined by liberty…" "We stand for the permanent hopes of humanity…" "…history has an author who fills time and eternity with its purpose…" "It is our task, the task of this generation to provide the response to aggression and terror…" "We did not ask for this mission, yet there is honor in history's call…" "let us move forward, confident , determined and unafraid…"

These are indeed words not only myself but most men and women of goodwill wanted to hear. As they echoed within the realm of my memory, I could not help reminding myself of the words of Ralph Waldo Emerson:

> What makes a nation's pillars high
> and it's foundations strong?

what makes it mighty to defy
the foes that round it throng?

It is not gold—its kingdoms grand
go down in battle shock
it's shafts are laid on sinking sand
not on abiding rock.

Is it the sword? Ask the red dust
of empires passed away:
the blood has turned their stones to rust
their glory to decay.

And is it pride? Ah that bright crown
has seemed to nations sweet—
but god has struck its luster down
in ashes at his feet.

Not gold but only men can make
a people great and strong—
men who for truth and honor's sake
stand fast and suffer long

Brave men who work while others sleep
who dare why other fly—
they build a nation's pillars deep
and lift them to the sky.

# PHOTO GALLERY

*With the late Senator John Tower of Texas, then chairman of the Senate Armed Services Committee, pointing to the strategic position of the Seychelles—on the oil route to Japan, Australia, and via the Cape to the United States.*

*The U.S. Airforce tracking station complex on top of Mahé Island, which during the Cold War gathered military intelligence over the Soviet Union.*

*Four-star General Zinni, who replaced Dessert Storm veteran General Schwarzkorf at the head of the U.S. Fifth Military Constituency, which covers the Middle East, South Asia, and Indian Ocean, pays a courtesy call on Seychelles vice president James Michel.*

*Seychelles is the nearest country to Diego Garcia. Port Victoria is therefore a favorite "rest and recreation" port for the U.S. Navy.*

The Bicentennial marking the 200th Anniversary of America's Independence was celebrated in the USA on July 4th 1976 with enormous enthusiasm and unprecedented fanfare. Five days before, on the 29th June 1976, the Seychelles had become an independent Republic with James R. Mancham as its first President. In no time the Seychelles Government issued a set of stamps to mark several milestones in US history. They were among the first Seychelles stamps to bear the effigy of President Mancham and they went a long way to testify to the prevailing friendship and understanding between the Republic of Seychelles and the United States of America.

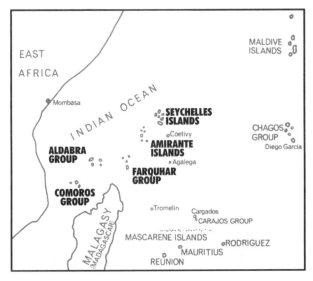

*Aldabra, Farquhar, and the Amirante Islands all form part of the Republic of Seychelles. Under the Law of the Sea Convention, the Republic of Seychelles has economic rights and jurisdiction over 200 miles around each of the 110 islands of its archipelago.*

*Greeting His Excellency, Ambassador Carl Stokes, the last U.S. ambassador to the Seychelles .*

*With Vice Admiral Charles W. Moore Jr., Commander of U.S. Naval Forces Central Command, Commander U.S. Fifth Fleet and Seychelles Chief of Staff, Colonel Leopold Payet on the USS* Johnhancock *during a goodwill visit to Port Victoria on Monday, December 13, 1999.*

*In Arusha, Tanzania (April 22, 1998) attending conference on "Leadership Challenges of Demilitarization in Africa." Front row, from L to R: myself, Uganda's Minister of Defence, H.E. the President of Tanzania, former President Oscar Arias of Costa Rica, and the vice president of Panama.*

To SIR James Mancham: Best wishes for a democratic and prosperous Seychelles. Herman J. Cohen assistant Secretary of State for Africa, WASHINGTON

*Posing with Herman Cohen, Assistant Secretary of State for Africa, prior to my return to Seychelles after more than fifteen years in exile.*

*Addressing the Heritage Foundation in Washington, D.C.*

*The U.S. Capitol in the background, with Washington lobbyist, Grover Norquist, who is President of the American for Tax Reform protesting against the decision of the U.S. government to close down its embassy in Seychelles.*

*In Washington, D.C., meeting with Speaker Newt Gingrich after the U.S. government had decided to close down its embassy in Seychelles.*

*With Florida Secretary of State Katherine Harris at a reception organized by The Foundation for Democracy in Africa in Miami in May 2000. Some weeks later, Mrs. Harris dropped a bombshell by refusing to allow a manual recount of votes in the election which ended with George W. Bush becoming the 43rd President of the United States.*

*With former Vice President Dan Quayle and H.E. former president of Madagascar, Mr. Albert Zaffy, with Mrs. Zaffy looking on at an IIFWP conference in Seoul in 2000.*

BUSH-CHENEY TRANSITION

Dear Sir James:

Thank you for your kind letter of congratulations on my election as President of the United States. I am honored by the choice of the American people and eager to take up the responsibilities of the office.

We will undoubtedly face a number of challenges in the years ahead. I am confident that, with a spirit of mutual respect, cooperation, and open dialogue, we can successfully meet these challenges. The future also presents enormous opportunities. Together we can use these opportunities to advance the peace, freedom, and prosperity of our peoples.

Please accept my best wishes to you and your family for the new year.

Sincerely,

George W. Bush

Sir James R. Mancham, K.B.E.
Former President of the Republic of Seychelles
Mahe

1800 G STREET NORTHWEST, WASHINGTON, D.C. 20270 • 202-513-7400

**THE SECRETARY OF STATE**

**WASHINGTON**

March 1, 2001

Dear Sir James:

Thank you for your letter and the copy of your book, *Oh Mighty America*.

The United States maintains an excellent working relationship with the Government of Seychelles. Although resident in Port Louis, Mauritius, our ambassador, Mark Erwin, understands that there is no substitute for personal contact and has made it a point to travel regularly to Seychelles.

I know we will continue to build upon the close ties our governments have sustained thus far.

Sincerely,

Colin L. Powell

His Excellency
    Sir James R. Mancham, KBE,
        Founding President of the
            Republic of Seychelles,
                P.O. Box 29,
                    Mahe, Seychelles.

**Serving the Nation, Serving the World:
Establishing Peace by Renewing
Families, Communities and Nations**

May 25–27, 2001     INTERNATIONAL SYMPOSIUM     New York,

*Designated with some others as an Ambassador for Peace by the IIFWP in accordance with its mission to establish world peace. Also in the photo: Dr. and Mrs. Sun Myung Moon, the founders of the IIFWP.*

*With the Hon. Zhou Guangzhao, vice president of the People's National Assembly of China in June 2001 at the People's Palace in Beijing. Also in the photo (on my right) Victoria's mayor, the Hon. Florence Benstrong and (on the left of Mr. Guangzhao) my wife, Catherine Olsen Mancham.*